JULIANUS POMERIUS

THE CONTEMPLATIVE LIFE

DE VITA CONTEMPLATIVA

Ancient Christian Writers

THE WORKS OF THE FATHERS IN TRANSLATION

EDITED BY

JOHANNES QUASTEN, S. T. D.
*Professor of Ancient Church History
and Christian Archaeology*

JOSEPH C. PLUMPE, Ph. D.
*Associate Professor of New Testament
Greek and Ecclesiastical Latin*

The Catholic University of America
Washington, D. C.

No. 4

JULIANUS POMERIUS

THE CONTEMPLATIVE LIFE

TRANSLATED AND ANNOTATED

BY

SISTER MARY JOSEPHINE SUELZER, Ph. D.

of the

Congregation of the Sisters of Providence
Saint Mary-of-the-Woods, Indiana

NEWMAN PRESS

New York, N.Y./Ramsey, N.J.

Nihil Obstat:

Johannes Quasten, S.T.D.
Censor Deputatus

Imprimatur:

Paulus C. Schulte, D.D.
Archiepiscopus Indianapolitanus
die 21 Junii 1947

Library of Congress
Catalog Card Number: 78-62457

ISBN: 0-8091-0245-5

PUBLISHED BY PAULIST PRESS
Editorial Office: 1865 Broadway, New York, N.Y. 10023
Business Office: 545 Island Road, Ramsey, N.J. 07446

PRINTED AND BOUND IN THE UNITED STATES OF AMERICA

CONTENTS

JULIANUS POMERIUS

THE CONTEMPLATIVE LIFE

INTRODUCTION

A scholar of note asserts that at the time when the glorious Church in Africa languished and perished, the illustrious bishop of Arles, St. Caesarius, saved Augustine's teaching and the fruits of his great doctrinal struggles, for Gaul and the Western Church in general; and he adds that Caesarius owed this accomplishment to his teacher, the African émigré Julianus Pomerius.[1] The same author claims for Pomerius the further distinction of having bequeathed to us the oldest pastoral instruction that survives in the West.[2] Most certainly, the master of Caesarius is to be credited with a place of honor in the survival and justification of Augustine's name and teaching; and the thoughtful reader of his one remaining treatise will not deny him his place in the early history of pastoral theology. But who other than patrologists and some few theologians even know the name Pomerius? There are, it is true, several translations of the *De vita contemplativa*, all of them now very old and none of them in English; but even the specialist finds it extremely difficult to locate one of these in our great libraries.

The name of Julianus Pomerius and what he wrote experienced a peculiar fate. For at least eight hundred years his *De vita contemplativa* was ascribed to St. Prosper of Aquitaine († after 455). It was not until the seventeenth century that his authorship was contested; but today it is universally conceded, although not absolutely proved, that the treatise is from the pen of Julianus Pomerius,[3] the last-recorded of the rhetors of Gaul.[4]

3

Little is known of Pomerius' life.[5] Born in Mauretania in North Africa, he migrated to Gaul [6] and opened a school of rhetoric in Arles. At some time around 497—the only date known with any certainty in Pomerius' life—he had as pupil Caesarius, the future bishop and saint of Arles.[7] Pomerius was ordained to the priesthood in Gaul,[8] but nothing is known of the time of his ordination or of his ecclesiastical career. He is addressed as *abbot* by one of his correspondents.[9] If this title is exact, it may have come from his directing at Arles an association of clerics living the common life,[10] as some passages of the *De vita contemplativa* appear to indicate.[11]

Pomerius attained considerable fame in his own lifetime. There are extant some letters written to him by Ruricius, bishop of Limoges,[12] who had become acquainted with him on a visit to Arles. In these letters he begs Pomerius to take up residence in Limoges [13] so that a new circle might benefit from his learning and piety. Not content with his repeated invitation to Pomerius, Ruricius wrote to Aeonius, bishop of Arles, imploring him to prevail upon Pomerius to move to Limoges.[13a] None of these letters produced any effect. Nor was Ruricius alone in attempting to persuade Pomerius to desert Arles for a new audience: Ennodius, the future bishop of Pavia, then a deacon, invited him to Italy,[14] but with no more success than Ruricius. Pomerius' worth is further witnessed by the continuator of Gennadius, who writes: " He is still living in a way of life worthy of God, suited to his profession and his rank." [15]

Four treatises are attributed to Pomerius: *De anima et qualitate eius;*[16] *De virginibus instituendis; De contemptu mundi et rerum transiturarum;* and *De vita contemplativa,* which alone has survived. Its preservation may have as ex-

planation the fact that at some time between the sixth and
the early eight century it began to be regarded as the work of
a more celebrated man, St. Prosper of Aquitaine. How the
error came about is not known; but it is easy to see that once
a treatise which contained high praise of St. Augustine [17]
had been mistakenly attributed to St. Prosper, the untiring
champion of the Bishop of Hippo, the ascription would find
ready acceptance. At any rate, from the time of Chrodegang († 766),[18] bishop of Metz, until the seventeenth century, whenever the De vita contemplativa is mentioned,[19]
it is attributed to St. Prosper. The Jesuit Jacques Sirmond
was the first to cast doubt upon the ascription to Prosper,[20]
basing his argument on a passage in the De vita contemplativa
(2. 9. 1) wherein, Sirmond claims, St. Hilary of Arles is
referred to as long dead, a reference that could not have been
made by St. Prosper since he survived St. Hilary by only some
sixteen years. The passage in question reads: " What did
the saintly Hilary do? Did not he also leave all his goods
to his parents or sell them and distribute the proceeds to the
poor? Yet, when because of his perfection he became bishop
of the church of Arles, he not only held what that church
owned at the time but also increased it by accepting numerous
legacies from the faithful. These most holy and perfect
bishops (St. Paulinus of Nola and St. Hilary), then, show
by plain deeds that what they did can and should be done."
It is debatable whether the lines just quoted imply that St.
Hilary had died a long time before they were written. They
seem barely to indicate that he was no longer alive when
they were composed; there is nothing to prevent their having
been written at some time in the sixteen or more years
between St. Hilary's death and St. Prosper's.

Cardinal Noris [21] argued more cogently against St. Prosper's authorship by pointing out that it is extremely unlikely that St. Prosper, ardent in his admiration for St. Augustine, would have praised St. Hilary as freely as the writer of the *De vita contemplativa* did in the passage already cited, since St. Hilary opposed St. Augustine's theology of grace whereas St. Prosper vigorously defended it. Besides, the Augustinism displayed in the *De vita contemplativa*—broad, moderate, and thoroughly practical in character [22]—is utterly different from that of St. Prosper. Moreover, an examination of the style of St. Prosper's genuine works and that of the *De vita contemplativa* reveals many dissimilarities.[23]

Conclusive proofs that Pomerius wrote the *De vita contemplativa* are the testimony of St. Isidore of Seville and the statement of authorship found in some of the oldest manuscripts. A further argument may be deduced from the nature of the other ascetical writings attributed to Pomerius: he was certainly qualified to write a work like the *De vita contemplativa*.

The testimony of Isidore is explicit: " He (Pomerius) also published three other books on the contemplation of the future life and on the way of the active life and also on the vices and the virtues." [24] Now, the résumé of the contents of the *De vita contemplativa*, as given in the foreword to Book 3, reads: " In the first volume I dealt with the contemplative life and the questions to what extent the active life differs from it and how you can with the help of God become a sharer in the contemplative virtue itself. In the second book I treated, by God's gift, what I thought should be said of the active life, too: I showed the usefulness of religious rebuke and the virtue of patience and the way the possessions of the Church should be administered and the manner of spiritual abstinence. Now it remains for me to undertake a discussion of the vices and the virtues, not relying on an endowment of which I am not conscious, but assisted by your prayers." This summary agrees exactly with the statement of Isidore.

Further, at least four of the oldest manuscripts of the *De vita contemplativa* bear the name of Pomerius as author. Sirmond himself saw two of these in the seventeenth century: one in the library of Charles de Montchal, archbishop of Toulouse; the other at Angers. P. Quesnel witnessed to the presence in the monastery of La Trappe of a copy of the treatise with Pomerius given as author. In the chapter library of the cathedral of Beauvais a very old codex is said to have existed, showing the same ascription.[25] Today no one seriously contests that Pomerius is the author of the work.[26]

The *De vita contemplativa* is an expression of the ideals of the contemplative and the active life, supplemented by a discussion of the vices and the virtues. Composed at the urgent request of a bishop, its first two books are directed to bishops, though the lessons inculcated apply to all clerics; the third book, as has been well said, addresses itself to every Christian.[27] The *editio princeps*[28] opens thus: " In the name of the most high Maker here begins the foreword of the book of the blessed Prosper on the contemplative life and the rule (*norma*) of ecclesiastics." At the close of the volume the phrasing is: " Here end the three books of Prosper, *doctor praeclarissimus*, treating concisely, in elegant style, subjects that are useful and necessary for everyone—on the contemplative life, that is, and on the active life and on the virtues and the vices." These titles are more descriptive than the short label currently in use;[29] but Schanz-Hosius-Krüger and Cayré[30] maintain that the present title, though seemingly pertinent to the first part of the work alone, really fits the whole, for the contemplative life, as Pomerius conceives it, is far from exclusive: it presupposes and motivates the active life; and since progress in the active life, essential to the attainment of the contemplative life, is brought about by growth in virtues, a discussion of the virtues and the vices rightly finds a place in a work on the contemplative life.

The date of the composition of the *De vita contemplativa* is unknown, but it can be assigned with probability to the close of the fifth century or the opening of the sixth. Scholars are agreed that it is the work of a mature and experienced person,[31] an inference borne out by Isidore, who places it last in his enumeration of Pomerius' writings.[32] One may gather from the nature of the treatise that Pomerius was already a priest when he composed it: it is not at all likely that the bishop who urged him to write would have asked a layman to treat of the duties of ecclesiastics; and Pomerius indicates his priestly rank when he expresses fear that clerical critics will accuse him of being traitorous in the charges he makes against worldly churchmen.[33]

The identity of the bishop Julianus at whose request the treatise was written and to whom it is dedicated cannot be established with any certainty. The name Julianus was very common in the fifth and sixth centuries. The conjecture that the addressee was Julianus, bishop of Carpentras, still seems preferable; it is favored especially by the nearness of Carpentras to Arles.[34]

The work's one claim to some originality—at least in the West—and to being a Latin classic lies in its instructing the bishops and, by implication, the clergy in general to combine in their ministry the active life and the contemplative. In this we have doctrine that goes back to the Greek philosophers, with whom the concept of activity and philosophic contemplation, of the βίος πρακτικός and βίος θεωρητικός, plays an important role. The School of Alexandria adopted and Christianized the idea of an active-contemplative life. Clement of Alexandria, for example, requires that every virtue be both active and contemplative. He stresses a permanent joining of Christian works and Christian *gnosis*, of what the philosophers termed activity (πράττειν) and contemplation (θεωρεῖν). He follows Plato, for whom perfection postulates activity as well as contemplation.[35] With Origen a clearer distinction is drawn between active and contemplative life, and his thinking on the subject is influenced much more by the Christian outlook.[36] Origen all but forgets the ancient provenience of this distinction and studies the Gospels for exemplifications of these two forms of life. He is the first to apply the famous Gospel episode of Martha and Mary to the problem: Mary symbolizes the contemplative life, Martha, the active life. Origen further came to the definite conclusion that the contemplative life is superior to the active, while Clement preferred a *vita mixta*.

The masters of the School of Alexandria, notably Origen, were certainly not unknown in Gaul.[37] However, the unique theme chosen by Julianus Pomerius was one that also occupied St. Augustine.[38] Whether the author was indebted to him in this matter or to the remoter Alexandrian prototypes, remains, like many other problems posited by Pomerius, to be investigated. Briefly, he develops his theme as follows: the union of the contemplative and the active life in the ministry is discussed in Book 1. The contents of Book 2 treat problems confronting those who aim at this union: their conduct towards sinners; their profitable use of the possessions of the Church; the excellence of detachment; the nature of abstinence. Pomerius' distinction between the active life and the contemplative is founded less on a manner of life than on states of soul—that of the soul which is seeking perfection (the active life) and that of the soul which possesses and enjoys it (the contemplative life). This conception, less exteriorized than the modern notion, is also more profound. It leads, moreover, to a union of the two ways of life, for the contemplative life perfects the active life without suppressing it.[39]

Pomerius teaches that the true and perfect contemplative life can be attained only in heaven through the beatific vision, but that even here below souls who have made the perfect renunciation obtain through hope a participation in the spiritual joys of the other life—a participation that is really a life of contemplation, but of a lower order. In his comparison of the active and contemplative life, both present and future, the author appears to identify the active life with the sum total of the efforts men must make to subdue their passions; but in the rest of the treatise the term is made to include all the efforts priests make to lead the faithful to the practice of virtue. The contemplative life here on earth, Pomerius teaches, is effected to some degree by meditation and the reading of the Scriptures; but the perfection of pastoral zeal may be taken as the sure proof that the contemplative life has been attained (1. 25. 1): " If holy priests . . . convert many unto God by their holy living and preaching; if they display no imperiousness, but do everything humbly; . . . if in the lives they live and in their preaching they seek not their own glory but Christ's; . . . if they console the afflicted, feed the needy, clothe the naked, redeem the captives, harbor strangers . . . : who will be such a stranger to faith as to doubt that such men are sharers in the contemplative virtue? "

In his treatment of the vices (Book 3), Pomerius recognizes only four capital sins: two of the first rank, pride and cupidity; and two less important, envy and vanity. Their remedies are fear of the Lord and charity. Of the four cardinal virtues he considers that three—temperance, justice, and fortitude—perfect the life of action; whereas prudence, which he associates closely with wisdom, the rule of the other virtues, perfects man in the order of practical reason, which guides him in all his actions. In connection with his treatment of justice, Pomerius produces (3. 28) a remarkably modern chapter on " social virtue "—*socialis virtus*—and the duty it imposes on those who are able to work for the good of society.

Much of Pomerius' teaching is inspired by St. Augustine, his professed model. His doctrine on the contemplative life does not go so far as St. Augustine's, but it, too, provides for a kind of vision of God, a feeble anticipation of the future vision. He follows St. Augustine also in tracing the vices to pride and their remedy to charity. Like St. Augustine he adopts the classic division of the four moral virtues and places prudence and wisdom in particular relief.

The style [40] of the *De vita contemplativa* is, for the most part, clear and smooth, more elegant than vigorous. There are passages that rise to eloquence; [41] but digressions and needless repetitions mar the quality of the work. This unquestionably is due in large part to the fact that Pomerius dictated the treatise. [42] The author repeatedly disclaims all learning and expresses contempt for showy declamation; [43] but his writing and his occupation as rhetor show that he was well-trained in the rhetoric of his age. [44] His knowledge of secular learning appears in his quotations from Terence, Cicero, and Vergil, and in his echoes from other authors. Moreover, it appears that he was conversant with Greek. [45] Pomerius' references to his own *rusticitas* are to be interpreted as an affectation of modesty—hardly more than rhetorical formulae—or as a manifestation of that strange fifth-century attitude towards secular learning that caused men like Ennodius to be converted from *belles lettres* as other men from sin.

*   *   *

The text used for the present translation is that of J. B. le Brun des Marettes and D. Mangeant, contained in S. *Prosperi Aquitani opera omnia* (Paris 1711) appendix 1-84, reprinted in ML 59 (Paris 1847) 415-520. Degenhart's collations of four rather inferior manuscripts [46] not used for the Paris edition have been examined, but none of the readings suggested by him for adoption appeared necessary or acceptable (but cf. below, 188 n. 18).

A French translation of the *De vita contemplativa* is reported by Ceillier. This is by J. Bouillon and was printed in Paris in 1576. A second French translation forms volume 8 of the series, *Le prêtre d'après les Pères* (Paris 1842), edited by J. M. Raynaud. J. G. Pfister's German translation, *Der heilige Prosper über das beschauliche Leben* (Würzburg 1826), as also Bouillon's French version, the present translator was unable to consult.

BOOK ONE

FOREWORD

For long have I stood firm against your wish, my Lord Julianus, most zealous of bishops. Not that I was obstinately stubborn, but I was conscious of my incompetence. For I thought, and perhaps the thought was justified, that even you could charge my presumption with improvident rashness, were I to undertake lightly and without any deliberation so great a work, one which ought surely to be treated painstakingly. Evidently, it behooved me first to assess the importance of the subject I was to discuss, and then, the Lord helping, if my talent upon examination held out the qualifications needed, to agree to undertake the task you imposed. Considering these and similar points with careful attention, I thought it necessary to hold myself a while from the presumption of writing. But because, as well as thinking of the difficulty of the work enjoined, I had to consider the authority of the one who enjoined it, neither did I wish to oppose you further, nor did I deem it right, being certain that your prayer, coming from the one who commissioned me, would give much greater aid to my abilities than the formidableness of the theme itself would burden them. The result was that my mind, diffident of its own capability, was encouraged to obey your command by this consideration: that it would not now be the part of humility to persist in silence, but rather of pride to refuse any longer the burden

13

placed on shoulders however weak. Though my inelegance [1]
made me incapable to assume this task, I trust, since you
imposed it, that I may be made capable through your confidence in me.

2. This, too, heartened me to give myself a trial: to
attempt great things would itself be great [2] even if nothing
were to result from one's discussion. For the treatment of
vital questions, though possibly not giving information to the
mind of him who fails to find what he is seeking, at least
exercises the talent of the investigator so that he learns by
seeking and not finding that he does not know what he
perhaps presumed he knew; and, as a result of being made
aware of his ignorance, he searches for what he has per-
ceived is lacking, preserves what he has found, and perseveringly makes use of what he has preserved; or if he has
been able to treat profitably and explain adequately, for
example, a passage proposed to him from Sacred Scripture,
he does not pride himself on his discovery of truth but glories
in the Lord, who has enlightened him inwardly to understand
the things on which he was to shed light. For, as learning
without the gift of God, which is charity, makes one conceited, so it edifies if charity is mingled with it. [3] And thus,
he who wishes to speak of God either says nothing and no
vanity carries him away; or if he does say something and is
convinced that he has received it from God, he has reason
to thank God and not to ascribe it proudly to the power of his
own talent.

3. But now I shall append the questions themselves in the
order in which you have proposed them for solution. You
bid me, then, to discuss in a few words the nature of the contemplative life and to explain as briefly as I can the difference

between it and the active life; whether one charged with ruling a church can become a sharer in the contemplative virtue; whether those who contemn the divine commands should receive calm toleration or should be reproved in proportion to their sins with ecclesiastical severity; whether it is expedient to hold the goods of the Church to provide for the community life of the brethren and their support,[4] or to spurn them through love of perfection; what should be regarded as perfection in abstinence, and whether it should be considered necessary only for the body or for the soul as well; to what extent simulated virtues differ from true virtues; from what prior causes and by what later additions vices usually are engendered and increased, and by what remedies, as by so many medicines, they can with God's help be lessened or corrected; in how many ways or degrees each virtue can be perfected; and whether there is truth in the theory of the philosophers which established four virtues as so many fountains of all virtues and also four vices as so many sources of all evils.[5] These, then, are the ten questions which you wanted me to explain, not that their exposition might afford you any knowledge, but rather that your zeal, should I properly discharge the task you imposed, might bring some edification to students of such matters by an explanation of these and similar questions. Of course, if you did not understand them, you would not have proposed them for elucidation in this formidable array. You wished me, nevertheless, to discuss things you already knew either that you might correct or reprove me if I should make any unreasonable exposition, or that at least through your care and my writing orthodox explanations could be made known to others. Accordingly, let me now discuss the nature of the contemplative life, the Lord helping me through your prayers.

TABLE OF CONTENTS

who is worried because he can neither abandon his church nor direct it, suggesting that he may rule it better by example. 18. It profits a priest little to show by example what should be done, unless by teaching he also indicates what must be believed. 19. The virtue of faith. Its province is not only to believe and to understand, but also to perform good works. 20. It avails a priest nothing to live a good life, if by his silence he does not correct him who lives a bad life. 21. The sad picture of a priest who lives carnally. 22. According to the statement of the Prophet they perish through their own fault who with a perverse will spurn the rebukes or admonitions of priests. 23. Priests, including those who can do otherwise, should teach so simply that all may understand what they teach. 24. The difference between teachers who edify the Church by teaching simply and those who vaunt their own eloquence by brilliant oratory. 25. Characteristics of priests who wish to become sharers in the contemplative life.

CHAPTER 1

The contemplative life is properly that life in which the Lord will be seen by the clean of heart.

1. The contemplative life, in which the intelligent creature, purified from all sin and restored in every part, is destined to see its Creator, takes its name from *contemplating*—that is, *seeing*. If this is so, that life in which God can be seen is to be regarded as contemplative. But in the present life, replete as it is with woes and mistakes, there is no doubt that God cannot be seen as He is. In the future life, then, which because of this is called contemplative, He is to be seen. And that is right: for, if to see God is supreme and

solid happiness, and if supreme happiness is regarded as the reward of the blessed, and if rewards are not given to those still fighting, but will be given after the triumph to those who have conquered: who does not understand that all the saints will see God in that everlasting life where they will rejoice without end? There will they rejoice where they will receive their reward; there will they receive their reward where they will triumph over enemies who are not only defeated but annihilated; there will they triumph where they will have no further adversary.

2. But in this life, however hard we struggle and with the help of the Lord lay low the throngs of enemies that surround us, yet if we do not want to be conquered, we shall never leave off fighting. Nor do battles already manfully fought out make of us conquerors who no longer have anything to fear; but the more do the foes' renewed attacks harass us. And so, since according to the saying of Holy Scripture *all human life is a trial upon earth,*[6] then will the trial end when the fight also ends; then will the fight end when after this life certain victory follows the fight, so that all soldiers of Christ [7] who to the end of their present life, aided from on high, untiringly resist their enemies may, when their wearisome journey in foreign parts has at last ended, reign happy in their homeland. There human nature will be so restored and so healed of every single infirmity that no sin will remain in it, nor will it any longer be able to sin. All this will be its reward: once it has been made partaker of the contemplative life, it will behold without satiety the Author of its happiness, rejoice in Him, obtain from Him that for which it has hoped, and remain forever in the state it has attained by holy living.

CHAPTER 2

The nature of the future life.

But now, what shall I say of the nature of that future life, which one ought rather to believe in than to speak of? And yet, so far as I can speak, I should not remain silent merely because I cannot say as much as I wish. Certainly, because we believe God to be ineffable,[8] we must not therefore refrain from saying what we can of Him. So, too, speak of that life we should, though more is believed than is put down in writing; for, plainly, not so much can be set forth in language as can be embraced by the soul; and the comprehension of the human mind, however profound, remains short of the full greatness of the reality itself. The future life, then, is believed to be happily everlasting and everlastingly happy, where there is true security, secure tranquillity, tranquil happiness, happy eternity, eternal happiness;[9] where there is perfect love, no fear, everlasting day, a blissful freedom of movement,[10] and one spirit in all secure in the contemplation of their God and in their abiding with Him; where that city[11] which is the blessed assembly of holy angels and men shines bright with splendid reward; where everlasting salvation abounds and truth reigns; where no one deceives or is deceived; whence none of the blessed is cast out and whither no evil one is admitted.

CHAPTER 3

The holy are to be separated from the wicked by the same judgment of God whereby formerly the blessed angels were separated from the unclean spirits.

1. And this also will happen, we believe, by the just judgment of God, whereby not only in recompense but also in location the just are to be separated from the unjust everlastingly: that those who are being rewarded will not come to the end of their reward, nor the damned, to the end of their punishment. For incorruptibility and immortality will be given also to the bodies of the damned in order that they may not come to the end of a punishment that is eternal, and that their penalty which is endless may not consume them but punish them. So, too, the bodies of the just will be endowed with blessed incorruptibility and immortality [12] that they may abide in glory and that everlasting glory may abide in them.

2. This judgment, which we say will take place between the just and the unjust, is the same, we believe, that was instituted between the holy and the unclean angels.[13] For, though they had been created without sin and had the happy commission of serving God, some of them, being corrupted of their own free will, did not wish to remain as they had been made; and when in a whirlwind of deadly pride [14] they had risen as enemies against their Creator, they were cast from the heights of heaven. These the judgment of God condemned with this punishment: namely, that since they did not wish to persevere when they could, they neither wish nor are able to be restored. For it was in the nature of their transgression that they were struck by the punishment of an

irrevocable judgment; and it surely was consonant with a condemnation utterly just that they lost completely the desire and the ability to be reinstated; just as it was, on the other hand, according to the will of the holy angels to remain in their high station when the wicked of their own accord fell; and it happened by divine and just judgment that their desire of remaining with God became the voluntary and happy necessity of abiding with Him always. And, therefore, because they have never sinned and no longer have the power to sin, having once been made participators in that contemplative life, they behold without satiety the Author of their happiness; and since they have been made everlastingly happy by reason of their steadfastness, they are secure in the permanence of their stay. They receive supreme and true joy from divine contemplation, in which they delight without being surfeited. Tirelessly and lovingly they serve their God, so perfectly happy that they neither desire to become happier, nor can they.

CHAPTER 4

The resurrection and the life of the saints.

1. This is the contemplative life, the blessed life; those who attain it by accomplishing good works will be like the blessed angels [15] and together with them will reign eternally with God. What they here believed there they will see; contemplating the essence of their Creator with clean hearts, they will rejoice with everlasting happiness; imbued with a divine and reciprocal love, they will be happily devoted to their God and to each other forever. When they have regained their bodies endowed with incorruption and immor-

tality,[16] they will receive citizenship in the heavenly homeland;[17] and, being made citizens forever,[18] they will obtain
the rewards promised them. There a happiness so great will
be showered upon them, so great will be their recompense of
heavenly delights, that they will thank the Author of their
reward for His great gifts and at the same time experience
no satiety from receiving blessings in such abundance. There
mind will be open to mind in the same manner that bodily
appearances are to bodily eyes, because there will be so great
and so perfect a sinlessness of men's hearts that they will
have reason to thank God, who made them sinless, and will
not have to blush because of the offensiveness of any stains
of sins; for neither sins nor sinners will be there, and those
who will be there will no longer be able to sin. No secrets
will then be hidden from the perfectly blessed who with
clean hearts [19] will see—and this is excellence far greater—
God Himself. Indeed, human beings will be so perfect
that they cannot further be changed for better or for worse.

2. This human substance, elevated to the likeness of its
Maker,[20] will recover in an improved state all the blessings
bestowed by nature which it had corrupted through sin:
understanding without error; memory without forgetfulness;
thought without wandering; charity without pretense; sensation without sin; soundness without weakness; happiness
without sorrow; life without death; facility without hindrance; abundance without satiety; and well-being in every
respect without disease. For whatever has here been harmed
in the human body, whatever wild beasts have bitten off,
or an unfortunate accident has taken away, or various diseases
have removed or human cruelty has cut off; or if fire or
anything else has produced any disability; or if old age,

troublesome even to the healthy, has caused the body to fail:
these and similar injuries to the body one resurrection will
there repair; and incorruptible soundness will preserve those
bodies which will have been renewed in all their members.[21]

3. Hence, all who will be there, though varying in rank
because of their varying merits, will, nevertheless, be happy
with one perfection; for each one's rewards will be sufficient,
and those already perfect cannot receive more than their
rewards. Just as satiety of the body leaves all equally sated
though individually persons may have taken not the same
amount of food but only according to their capacity, so all
the saints, though distinguished by some difference in their
levels, will be perfect with one happiness because they will
also be happy with one perfection. Besides, in that place
of such happiness no one will arrogate greater merit to himself, because no arrogance will exist there; nor will he who is
lower be envious of the one above him, because no envy is
possible there. And thus, although a diversity of mansions [22]
will exist there, yet there will be the greatest equality of one
perfection in those who will have one happiness of the
heavenly kingdom.

CHAPTER 5

*The happiness of the contemplative life even here below
delights those who contemn the things of the world.*

1. That man longs to merit this happiness who renounces
all present things for the sake of the things to come, and,
being lifted from domestic cares, which sometimes hinder
the progress of those trying to live perfectly, to that sublimity
of divine contemplation, overcomes even the very affections

of his flesh. By despising all things below, which very often cast to earth souls that feel secure by reason of the sanctity of their past life, he even approaches things celestial; and he is carried as much nearer to divine things as he ascends above all things human through a desire of perfection. He is confident that if with uncompromising will he prefers the contemplative life here to uncertain honors, wealth with the anxiety that it brings, and ephemeral delights, he will find true honors, wealth without care, and eternal delights when he has arrived at the perfection of the contemplative virtue in that blessed life where he will be by God's reward. Indeed, who will be more honorable than he whom the divine mercy has blessed with dignity equal to the angels'? [23] Who will be richer than he whom the ineffably abounding happiness of the heavenly kingdom has enriched? Or what even here is more delightful than divine contemplation, which fills those who truly yearn for it with the incorruptible sweetness of the future reward? For, in truth, the contemplative life even on earth delights its lovers by a consideration of future blessings and illumines with the gift of spiritual wisdom those who devote themselves to it with the whole bent of their minds, as far as can be done in this life; and by means of a certain incentive for reaching perfection it sets them aglow for that fullness of the divine vision of which they, intent upon their desire for heaven, have hope, so that what they now behold in obscurity [24] and do not completely discern they may then see in that revelation.[25]

CHAPTER 6

The perfection of the contemplative life which is possible here below cannot be compared to its future perfection.

1. Therefore, I have not so spoken of the sublimity of the contemplative life in the future, where perfection is to be perfected, as to say that in the present life it cannot be secured by all who despise the world, if only they turn to it with entire zeal; if, burning with a desire for it, they scorn the enticements of the present, and, made much too strong to be ensnared by worldly occupations, apply themselves to meditation on divine subjects and the future promises. But if we consider the statement of the Apostle Paul wherein he distinguishes between that knowledge which is here and that which will exist there, saying: *We know in part and we prophesy in part,*[26] we cannot and should not compare the divine contemplation which is in this life with that of the future life; for the same Apostle adds: *But when that which is perfect is come*—meaning in that life—then *that which is in part shall be done away.*[27] And thus, what we now understand in part we shall then, when we have been brought to that fullness of divine contemplation, see perfectly.

2. And yet, because there all things will be comprehended, not piecemeal, but together and entirely, one should not on that account despair of at least some knowledge in this frail body. For, although *the corruptible body is a load upon the soul, and the earthly habitation presseth down the mind that museth upon many things,*[28] still, so far as is possible, the human mind, which its Creator made to His own image, should strive even here to see God intellectually by faith so

that it may see Him more fully when by His gift it attains the vision of its Maker. Note how strikingly the holy Apostle distinguishes between faith and sight when he says: *We walk by faith, not by sight.*[29] Faith, then, it is by which one walks, and sight it is which is seen; for in this life, where we advance through faith by right living, we walk, as it were, by the steps of our good works. In the future life, however, where we shall attain sight, there will no longer be a place to which we may walk as though advancing farther; but we shall see with insatiable delight that vision to which we have come by walking spiritually through faith.

CHAPTER 7

The holy can see God perfectly only after attaining the happiness of the future life.

1. Therefore, those who fully desire it and with God's help are capable of it are so to be encouraged to the contemplative life as to be mindful that the perfection of the divine contemplation itself is reserved for that blessed life which is to come; that there they may see God perfectly as He is where they themselves will also be made perfect by attaining eternal life and the heavenly kingdom. But if in this life human frailty could have perfectly contemplated the essence of God, never would the holy Evangelist have said: *No man hath seen God at any time.*[30] He did not say: "No one will see Him." To show plainly, then, that the sight of God was not refused holy men but deferred, what he denied for the present time he promised for the future, saying: *Blessed are the clean of heart, for they shall see God.*[31] Nor did he say here: "For they see God." Conse-

quently, if God, who in this life neither in the past nor present could be seen without the assumption of some form, is to be seen in the future life, there the perfection of divine contemplation is to be hoped for where there will be the fullness of all good things.

CHAPTER 8

The nature and degree of perfection of the contemplative life in this flesh; and how those who despise the world apply themselves to the enjoyment of that life.

1. Let the pursuer of the contemplative life, then, approach his Creator to be enlightened in heart; let him watchfully serve Him by contemplating Him and untiringly enjoying Him; let him desire Him continually; for love of Him let him flee all that could turn Him away; let him rest all his thoughts and all his hope on His pleasure. Let him take time for holy meditations on the Sacred Scriptures; let him, being divinely illumined, delight in them. There let him consider his whole being as in some gleaming mirror; let him correct what he sees disordered; let him hold to what is right; reform what is deformed; cultivate what is beautiful; preserve what is sound; by careful reading strengthen what is weak. Let him not tire of reading the commandments of his Lord, love them without growing weary, fulfill them efficaciously; and, being adequately instructed by them, let him understand what he should avoid and what he should pursue. Let him devote himself to an examination of the mysteries of the same Divine Scriptures, read of Christ there prophesied,[32] see Him represented, understand the perdition of the

3 ‘

reprobate people according to prophecy, mourn its fulfillment, rejoice in the salvation of the Gentiles. Let him hold fast the things that were predicted and accomplished in the past; let him trust future promises. Far removed from the noise of worldly concerns, let him ardently ponder those things whereby he may inflame his soul to a desire of his future reward. Let him be intent on spiritual studies, which may make him better and better from day to day; let him love holy leisure, in which he may conduct the business of his soul. Let him count the earth as dead to him, and let him show himself crucified to the enticements of an alluring world.[33] Let him place the vision of his Creator incomparably above delight in present spectacles. Always let him raise himself by advancing stages to the summit of divine contemplation; never, not even for a moment, let him turn from the consideration of promises for the future to look back upon things of earth.[34] Let him constantly direct the gaze of his mind to the place he desires to attain; let him place before the eyes of his soul the happiness of the future life,[35] and let him love it. Let him neither dread nor desire anything temporal; let neither fear of losing temporal possessions nor greed of gaining them weaken the resolution of his mind. Let not prosperity corrupt nor adversity shake him.[36] Let not favorable opinion arouse his vanity nor unfavorable opinion depress him; let not misplaced criticism or praise increase his happiness or take away from it. Let him not rejoice at all in temporal matters, nor grieve. Unconquered in joy and sorrow, let him preserve the mien of a steadfast soul; let nothing the world promises or threatens shake the stable firmness of his heart; but, remaining always the same and natural, let him not feel the loss or the gain of this world.[37] And when he, prompted by a desire of the contemplative life, has fulfilled these and similar injunctions, let him unwaveringly believe that he has not been entirely perfected here but that he will be perfected in that blessed future life, and let him tend towards it, where he will be able to see the essence of God with face unveiled.

CHAPTER 9

There is as much difference between the perfection of this life and the future as between the perfect who are unwilling to sin and those who can no longer sin.

1. Now, just as here in a comparison of the just someone is called perfect because the just man obeys precepts but the perfect man goes beyond them, so the latter, when compared to those who will be absolutely perfect in the blessed life, is not, so to say, perfectly perfect. Though all his guilt has been absolved, his weakness has not yet been cured, but it is in the process of being cured; and, therefore, though he commits no sin so that he may be truly perfect, he has, nevertheless, the power to sin because he has not been healed by the removal of all weakness; and so, too, being cleansed from all sin, there where he will not be able to sin he will be perfectly whole and supremely perfect.

2. Here, moreover, however much a man is eminent for the excellence of his sanctity, however much he excels by the eminence of perfection, he can, it is true, become perfect according to the capacity of this life, but he is not so secure in his perfection that he need not be careful of a fall; and, surely, where anyone is in anxiety, happiness is not absolute. Happiness should not at all be counted perfect if it is not secure; and it will be secure only when eternal security will have taken anxiety away.[38] Therefore, if men are called

happy in this life, they are happy in the hope of future happiness.[39] Actually, however, not here but in that life will they be happy; for there the happiness of all the blessed will indeed be perfect where human nature, made perfectly happy, will see its Creator's glory and its own and will cling to Him without any fading of its happiness.

CHAPTER 10

On earth the holy saw God in a created form which He assumed.

Let it not affect the argument that we read that here, too, God was seen by just men of old; for He was not seen in this our lowly state as He will be seen in that glorification. Indeed, without the form of a visible creature, in which He appeared when and to whom of the just He willed according to the dispensation of the times,[40] neither could He have been seen, nor would this be possible now; but we shall be able to see Him when our pilgrimage has taken us to our homeland above, and when blessed immortality has clothed our mortality, and when faith itself, by which we here believed in the future, has been fulfilled and has led all the truly faithful to the contemplation of God and the possession of heavenly rewards.

CHAPTER 11

The nature of the glorified bodies which are to be in the resurrection.

There the bodies will be of different sexes, it is true, but without any bodily concupiscence. Then perfect love will exist among all and no cupidity.[41] Then, too, nothing of

visible creation will escape bodily eyes because the vision of
incorruptible bodies will undoubtedly be incorruptible; and
it will be incomparably swifter than here so that nothing
visible can be shut off from it. In fact, bodies endowed with
immortality are to shed whatever retards them, but nothing
of their integral being; need will be taken away, not volition,
with the result that without delay of time or hindrance of
weight they will be there where they wish to be; and so,
without any difficulty the body, then spiritualized, will follow wherever the spirit wishes to go, perfect with the equality
of the angels' happiness. Then no regret over children,
parents, or spouses not found there can sadden the blessed,[42]
because the excellence of that happiness does not recognize
the names of all bodily relationships which our frailty here
possessed. There all, whoever they are, will be one body;
and each one will rejoice in his own and everyone else's
happiness. Let these words on the contemplative life suffice.

CHAPTER 12

The difference between the contemplative life and the active.

1. Now let me briefly discuss what the difference is between the contemplative life and the active. In order that
it may be quite clear, let me compare the two lives: the contemplative, that is, and the active, bringing out their virtues.
It pertains to the active life to advance in the midst of human
affairs and to restrain the rebellious movements of the body
by the rule of reason; to the contemplative, to ascend above
things human by the desire of perfection and constantly to
devote oneself to the increase of virtues. The active life is

the journeying; the contemplative is the summit. The former makes a man holy; the latter makes him perfect. It is characteristic of the active life to inflict injuries on no one; of the contemplative, to bear inflicted injuries calmly. Nay, to state this more precisely, one who fulfills the requirements of the active life is prompt to forgive the man who has sinned against him; one who follows the contemplative life is prepared rather not to notice than to pardon the offenses by which he is attacked but not at all affected. The former controls anger by the virtue of patience; places the bridle of moderation on unrestrained passions; is touched by carnal desires but does not consent; is smitten by the curiosity of this world but is not carried away; is shaken by the attacks of the devil but is not overcome; and, being subject to his God with a devoted mind, is not worn down but proved by diverse temptations. The follower of the contemplative life by holy virtues overcomes all the feelings which variously affect the life of mortals; free from all desires and disturbances, he enjoys blessed quiet; and, being made superior to his temptations and passions by reason of his untrammeled mind, he is raised on high by the indescribable joy of divine contemplation. The follower of the active life, by harboring the stranger, clothing the naked, governing the subject, redeeming the captive, protecting him who is oppressed by violence, is continually cleansing himself from all his sins and enriching his life with the fruits of good works. The other, having given his possessions for the use of the poor, in one act divests himself of the world and raises himself to heaven with all his strength. He casts the things of the world upon the world and delivers himself up with a devoted mind to Christ, of whom he asks that immortal riches be given him as a poor man; begs daily to be protected as one weak; desires to be clothed with the garment of immortality [43] as one naked; prays to be defended from the attacks of invisible enemies as one oppressed by the frailty of the flesh; and desires that the land of heaven be given him as one who is a stranger.

2. The active life has an anxious course; the contemplative, everlasting joy. In the former a kingdom is being acquired; in the latter it is received. The active life causes men to knock at the gate as though with the hands of good works; the contemplative life calls into their homeland those who have completed their course. In the former the world is contemned; in the latter God will be seen; and, to pass over many things I have not the power to mention, those who in this active life have triumphed over the evil spirits will in that contemplative life, which is supremely happy, become by God's reward equal to the holy angels and will reign forever happy with Him in that city above.

And thus, because I have already said much of the contemplative life in the foregoing and because the second book will contain what is to be said of the active life, let these statements suffice so that in the discussion to follow I may consider the other matters, too, which I will treat with the third question as my theme up to the end of this book. Let us now consider whether one charged with ruling a church can become a sharer in the contemplative life.

CHAPTER 13

Holy priests can become sharers in the contemplative life.

1. One who diligently considers what I have previously said about the contemplative life and who, being adequately instructed, understands when and where its perfection can

be attained will not doubt that princes of the churches can and should become followers of the contemplative life; for, whether, according to the opinion of some, the contemplative life is nothing but the knowledge of future and hidden things; or whether it is freedom from all occupations of the world; or the study of Sacred Scripture; or what is recognized as more perfect than these, the very vision of God: I do not see what objection can be brought forward to prevent holy priests from attaining the four things I have mentioned. Of course, two of them, the first and the last—namely, the knowledge of hidden and future things and the very vision of God—will be incomparably more excellent in that blessed life than in this, enmeshed as it is in diverse errors, since the knowledge of all things as well as the very essence of God will be fully and perfectly apprehended. But the two between—that is, freedom from all occupations of the world and the study of Sacred Scripture—bishops [44] can have even here; but those who on separating themselves from all the entanglements of world affairs do not grow sluggish in idleness but pursue the business of their perfection and who, turning from the folly of worldly wisdom, untiringly devote themselves to the Word of God, become truly wise, have knowledge of heavenly matters, despise worldly affairs, refute the opponents of sound doctrine, instruct the obedient, apply themselves to holy virtues by which they may each day become closer to God, and, eager for their own improvement as well as for that of all their disciples, receive even here some taste, as it were, of the contemplative life, whereby they are more keenly stimulated to it. But there, having been made lastingly happy, they will rejoice in its perfection. Accordingly, they are not made vain because here they are honored as leaders of all faithful Catholics; but they rejoice rather that there they will be more distinguished members of Christ, who is the Head of priests and of all the faithful.

2. But if, God forbid, entangled by worldly business, they extend the boundaries of their estates without limiting their covetousness [45] and give themselves everywhere to choice delights which weaken soul and body; if they seek not the glory of Christ [46] but their own, deceived by the honors of the fawning crowd, and believe what others say of them rather than believe their own conscience; if they place all their joy not in their future reward nor in sanctity of life but in their rank alone and, although they love to be what they are believed to be, are never dissatisfied with themselves, and, because they are content with themselves, are not solicitous for their improvement: who does not see that such men, if they continue in such conduct and do not correct themselves before the end of their present life, cannot share in the contemplative life? Only those attain it who have made efforts to be what they have become; who strive not to seem, but to be, what they are; who are distinguished not by the praise of others but by their own conduct, conspicuous not only because of their own rank but more because of the nobility of their priestly life; who are bishops not by title only but by virtue—men fit for the contemplative life, and coheirs of the joys of heaven.[47]

CHAPTER 14

The writer explains that he does not make bold to teach the teachers of the Church.

And lest my words appear presumptuous to anyone if they portray what all priests should not be or should be, I think that I ought to speak not of the generality but of a single person and preferably of you, who rashly—permit me to say it—imposed on me the duty of a precarious discussion. Nor should I treat points unknown to you but the usual ones which we are wont to consider in our conversations together. After this brief declaration, I think that no one can justly impute rashness to my quoting any more than to my argument, as though I were daring to teach my fathers,[48] from whom I am ready to receive and to learn the pattern of living.

CHAPTER 15

The negligence of the priest who, because he acts contrary to his preaching, cannot fill the role of teacher.

Consider, then, the most serious things you were wont to say, while I listened with approval, of the administration of a bishop who, putting in second place the care of the people entrusted to him, desires the goods of this life more ardently than those of the afterlife, and, unmindful that he must give an account to the Sheperd of all shepherds[49] not only of himself but also of the flock entrusted to him, gives no thought to his own ruin and that of his charges. The sins of the erring do not sadden him, nor do the gains of those making progress bring him joy; but, being solicitous of himself alone, and, moreover, often not even of himself, he has no interest in the good or evil that his charges do. He does not preach perseverance to the just, penance to the wicked, contempt of the world to the converted, future punishment to the estranged. He cannot say to those who disregard his warning: "Think of the future judgment"—a thing which he himself perchance does not consider; to those who love the world: "Love not the world," if love of the world delights him; to the ambitious: "Give up your ambition," if ruinous ambition carries him away; to drunkards: "Beware of drunkenness," if he swills wine to the point of losing his senses. Stuffed with sumptuous dinners, he cannot recommend to his charges the abstinence he spurns; addicted to the vice of covetousness, he cannot dissuade the avaricious from a love of money; holding fast to enmities, he will lack the courage with priestly calm to reconcile the minds of those at variance; he blushes to preach to judges the justice which he himself corrupts in favor of a powerful person; he does not defend the oppressed if he either honors or despises individuals. Whatever good he omits he will not order to be done, and whatever evil he commits he will not forbid to be done because by his own contradictory action he either loses or lessens the authority that must be his as a teacher.

CHAPTER 16

The danger that awaits those who either wish to abandon the church entrusted to them or neglect to direct it zealously.

When you called to mind these and similar things, you were sorry that you had accepted a bishopric, which, just as it sheds lustre upon its administrator if it is well managed, so, too, condemns him who neglects it. When you wished in consequence to abandon the church entrusted to you, as if unequal to rule it, and to withdraw to some solitary spot, not so much from a desire for rest as from despair of fulfilling your charge, nothing forced you to change your decision for the better except your fear of incurring a greater danger. For, if it is dangerous not to steer a ship cautiously through the waves, how much more dangerous is it to abandon it storm-tossed to the swelling billows? Though it is better not to enter such a ship, once a man has taken it over, it behooves him to cast away fear of the stormy sea, and, taking hope of reaching shore, to steer into port without any loss of cargo. Since this comparison pleased you, I added: "And so a church, which sails the sea of the world like a great ship,[50] which is buffeted by various waves of temptations in this life, tossed to and fro by the attacks of unclean spirits as though by stormy waves, dashed against the rocks and shoals of scandals, hemmed in as if by a reef of heavy sand, should not be deserted but should be directed. Just as it will bring all its passengers safely to port when it is controlled by the watchfulness of its pilot, so it will cause the loss not only of its passengers but also of the pilot himself if it is swamped by the waves or set adrift."

CHAPTER 17

An appeal to one who is worried because he can neither abandon his church nor direct it, suggesting that he may rule it better by example.

As I proceeded with these and similar points, you were deeply moved and grieved that you had been reduced to this necessity: you could neither discharge your office with any zeal nor abandon it without sin. And then I felt compassion with your holy sighs because of that affection of heart which binds me to you, and I told you that by praying you could accomplish what you could not effect by teaching; that faithful Catholics usually profit more by good example than by brilliant words; [51] and that the best and perfect teaching is that which a spiritual way of life exemplifies, not that which empty speech utters; and that on Judgment Day we shall be asked not for words but for deeds; that it is scarcely possible to persuade what the tongue teaches if one's life does not accord with one's tongue; that, on the other hand, it is possible to gain approval, whether you preach or not, for what you establish as worthy by deeds and impress on people disposed to follow an example, as something they can find delight in achieving. You derived some relief from my suggestions; and forthwith you replied, if I remember correctly, as follows:

CHAPTER 18

It profits a priest little to show by example what should be done, unless by teaching he also indicates what must be believed.

" Even if all perfection were to consist in deed alone and not also in faith and if a man were to be asked on Judgment Day not what he had believed but what he had done, who would be so presumptuous as to flatter himself on his justice if he had disregarded the importance of the Church's doctrine? For we ought not only, according to the Apostle, to show an example to the faithful [52] but also to teach those faithful who have been divinely entrusted to us for instruction: of the Father, how He is held to be the only unbegotten One; of the Son, how He is generated from the Father; of the Holy Spirit, how He, proceeding from the Father and the Son, can be called neither unbegotten nor begotten; how these three are one, and how this one is not divided but is distinguished into three; and how neither the Father nor the Holy Spirit, but only the Son, born ineffably of the Father alone, took on complete human nature without any change of His substance; and how He proved Himself true God and man by His virtues and His sufferings; allowed Himself to be captured; willed to be put to death; arose on the third day; by His own power raised into heaven the humanity He had taken from us; by the example of His resurrection gave us, reborn in Him, the hope of rising happily; made us His members; [53] threatened with punishment not those who believe in Him but those who abandon Him; [54] and promised His adherents the kingdom of heaven.[55]

CHAPTER 19

The virtue of faith. Its province is not only to believe and to understand, but also to perform good works.

" These and other things a priest should know in order to teach, and the people should believe in order to understand what is taught, as the Apostle says: *Unless you believe you will not understand.*[56] From this it may be gathered that faith does not come from reason, but reason comes from faith; nor does he who understands believe, but he who believes understands; and he who understands does good, as is written elsewhere: *He would not understand that he might do well.*[57]   He did not say ' could not,' but ' would not understand,' so that we may know that the phrase ' to be unwilling to understand ' is nothing but ' to be unwilling to believe.'   Therefore, in order that anyone may do good, let him be zealous to understand; and let him believe in order that he may understand.   But because the same Apostle says: *Faith cometh by hearing, and hearing by the word of God,*[58] a teacher of the Church ought to preach what the one about to believe should hear; for without preaching there will of course be no hearing, as the same Apostle attests, saying: *How shall they hear without a preacher?* [59] If, then, no one hears without a preacher; if without hearing he does not believe; if without faith he does not understand; if without understanding he does not do good: the word of faith should be preached so that hearing he may believe, believing he may understand, and understanding he may do good perseveringly. For he who can use the choice of free will is justified neither by works without faith nor by faith alone without works.[60] And, therefore, if *with the heart we believe unto justice, but with the mouth confession is made unto salvation,*[61] the unbeliever, by not having faith, will be able to have neither justice of heart nor salvation.

CHAPTER 20

It avails a priest nothing to live a good life, if by his silence he does not correct him who lives a bad life.

" However, what will the Apostle's saying avail—namely, that we should give example to the faithful,[62] if he who has been charged with exhorting the good and reproving the bad, by living well shows himself to the good for imitation but by his silence does not correct the bad? For, if I am not mistaken, on this account a priest must live a holy life: that he may not make his words void by inconsistent acts if he does not do what he preaches should be done, or if he has presumed to preach what he does not do. But if he has acted otherwise,[63] he accomplishes nothing among those who know his life because he has been appointed over a church of

God for this purpose: not only by living a good life to instruct others by the example of his manner of life, but also by preaching faithfully to set each one's sins before his eyes; to show what punishment awaits the obdurate, what glory is in store for the obedient; to neglect no one's salvation through despair; to mourn for the souls of those who are unwilling to be corrected, imitating the Apostle, who says: *I mourn many of them that sinned before and have not done penance;* [64] and again: *Who is weak and I am not weak? Who is scandalized, and I am not on fire?* [65]

2. "Therefore, since he knows that if he spares the rich and the powerful, if he even favors those who live a bad life, he causes their ruin and at the same time perishes himself, he should both live a holy life because of the example he must give, and teach because of the charge of his ministry, being certain that his personal justice will not avail him from whose hand a doomed soul is required. When any other person who has no obligation to teach perishes, he alone will pay the penalty of his crime; but he who has the commission of dispensing the word, however holy the life he lives, if he is either embarrassed or afraid to reprimand those who live wickedly, perishes with all who are lost through his silence. And what will it profit him not to be punished for his own sin if he is to be punished for another's? If I am not mistaken, this is what the Lord states through the Prophet Ezechiel under the threat of some fear, when he says to him: *So thou, O son of man, I have made thee a watchman to the house of Israel.* [66] Nor should we give passing heed to the fact that He calls a priest a ' watchman.' It is the work of a watchman to look out from a higher place and to see more than all others: so, too, a priest should stand out above all by the sublimity of his pattern of life and should have the

attraction of a superior knowledge of the way of life whereby he may be able to instruct those who live under him.

3. " Let us now see what the Word of God has on this. *Thou shalt hear the word from my mouth*, He says, *and shalt tell it them from me.* [67] that is to say, a priest should speak what he has learned from divine reading, what God has inspired in him, not what he has invented by the suppositions of his human understanding. *Thou shalt tell it them from me*, He says: ' from me, not from yourselves, shall you speak my words. You have no cause to be proud of them as though they were your own.' ' From *me*,' He says, ' tell them.' And now let us hear what he should announce: *When I say to the wicked: O wicked man, thou shalt surely die: if thou dost not speak to warn the wicked man from his way, that wicked man shall die in his iniquity, but I will require his blood at thy hand.*[68] What could be said more clearly, more patently? ' If,' He says, ' you have not spoken to the impious that he should guard himself from his impiety, and he should die, *I will require his blood at thy hand.*' That is to say, ' If you do not tell him his sins, if you do not reprove him *that he may be converted from his wickedness and live,*[69] I shall cause both you who did not rebuke him and him who sinned because you were silent, to be lost in everlasting flames.' Who, I ask, will have so stony a heart, who will be so unfeeling,[70] that this judgment does not frighten him? Who will be so far from faith that he does not believe this judgment?

CHAPTER 21

The sad picture of a priest who lives carnally.

1. " But as long as we, seduced by temporal things, seek in this life our profit and honor, we strive to be not better than others but richer, not holier but more honored. We do not think of the flock of the Lord which has been entrusted to us to feed and guard, but we think carnally of our own pleasure, of power, riches, and other allurements. We wish to be called shepherds without making any effort to be such. We shun the labor of our office, seek its dignity. We do not beat off the beasts of unclean spirits who are tearing the flock; and we ourselves consume what is left by them when we not only do not reprove but even reverence rich or influential sinners for fear that they, being offended, may not direct their usual gifts to us or may withdraw the favors we desire. And so, captivated by their gifts and favors, nay, enslaved to them because of these things, we shrink from speaking to them of their sinfulness or of the judgment to come. And for that reason the Word of God pounds at our pride with warnings, but our hearing gives no admittance to anything whereby we may profit; for, held captive by the sweetness of the present life, we have no desire to consider what everlasting punishment awaits our negligence.

2. " Against shepherds, then, on whose empty name we delude ourselves, these things are said: *Thus saith the Lord: Woe to the shepherds of Israel, that fed themselves. Should not the flocks be fed by the shepherds? You ate the milk, and you clothed yourselves with the wool; you killed that which was fat; but my flock you did not feed. The weak*

*you have not strengthened, and that which was sick you have
not healed. That which was broken you have not bound up;
that which was driven away you have not brought again;
neither have you sought that which was lost; but you ruled
over them with rigor and with a high hand. And my sheep
were scattered because there was no shepherd; and they became the prey of all the beasts of the field.*[71] And a little
later: *Therefore, ye shepherds, hear the word of the Lord:
As I live, saith the Lord God, forasmuch as my flocks have
been made a spoil, and my sheep are become a prey to all
the beasts of the field because there was no shepherd; for
my shepherds did not seek after my flock, but the shepherds
fed themselves and fed not my flock. Therefore, ye shepherds, hear the word of the Lord: Thus saith the Lord:
Behold, I myself come upon the shepherds. I will require my
flock at their hand, and I will cause them to cease from feeding the flock any more; neither shall the shepherds feed
themselves any more.*[72]

3. " Who would not tremble at these words? Who would
hear them without insufferable fear of the judgment to come
except one who either does not understand or does not believe in what is to come? But because God so openly revealed
what He wished to be carried out and so strengthened it with
the authority of His name that it might be easier to contemn
such evident and divine things—and this it is wrong even to
say—than to pretend not to understand or not to believe them,
when we hear, *Thus saith the Lord*: who except one who
does not believe in God does not believe that it will be as the
Lord says? As for the statement: *Woe to the shepherds*,
who except one who does not consider the future does not
understand that this ' woe ' was placed as a curse and that

he means us by the word 'shepherds'? Being made shepherds, we undertook to feed the sheep of the Lord; and we feed ourselves when we do not look to the good of our flock but attend to that which promotes and increases our own pleasures. We receive the milk and wool of Christ's sheep, enjoying the daily offerings and tithes of the faithful; and we lay aside the care of feeding and refreshing our flocks, by whom in unnatural order we expect to be fed. We do not cure by spiritual advice the man who is sick because of his sins; we do not give strength or relief by our priestly help to the man who is broken by diverse tribulations; we do not call back the wanderer to the way of salvation; we do not seek with a shepherd's solicitude the man already lost through despair of pardon. We have become men of power only for this end: that we might assume a tyrannical rule over our subjects—not that we might defend the afflicted from the violence of the powerful who rage against them like wild beasts.

4. "Hence it is that some are lost, being grievously harassed not only by the powerful of this world but also—which is worse—by us. These it is the dire warning of the Lord that He will require at our hand, when He says: *I will require my sheep at the hand of the shepherds; and I will cause them to cease feeding them any further*. What does this mean but: 'I will deprive those shepherds who feed themselves, not my flock, of their sublime dignity and cast them away among the reprobate because they did not want to guard their honor'? Because I was terrified by the consideration of these and similar things, *fear and trembling are come upon me, and darkness hath covered me; and I said: 'Who will give me wings like a dove, and I will fly and be*

at rest? ' [73] And this is the full account of why I wept, thinking of my inexperience and my future end; and I wished to lay down the burden of my bishopric and to withdraw and flee, to remain in solitude and there await the Lord, who would save me [74] from my troubled heart and from the storm of my unbearable anxieties."

CHAPTER 22

According to the statement of the Prophet they perish through their own fault who with a perverse will spurn the rebukes or admonitions of priests.

1. To this I then replied: "You utter these things with bitter lamenting, and you exaggerate to the offense of bishops or, at least, of the episcopal dignity, as though in that place where you read those things which rightly alarmed you there were not also other passages which, since you overlooked them, I shall touch upon briefly in defense of the sacerdotal office. [75] After those words with which the Prophet indicates the end of negligent priests, he speaks thus of the bishop who shows concern for his office: *But if thou tell the wicked man that he may be converted from his ways, and he be not converted from his way, he shall impiously die in his iniquity; but thou hast delivered thy soul.* [76] Here, certainly, it is shown with sufficient clarity that, whether their hearers profit or not, priests should not be silent before them; that they are not on that account guilty if the people by chance do not hear their words or if they despise them after hearing them; but that they are guilty if they refrain from correcting them. For, if obstinate persons when admonished do not derive advantage either from the example of their pastors' lives or

from the words of their doctrine, they are the cause of their own ruin; and in their sins they surely cannot involve their teachers, whose examples and words they despised.

2. " This thought the same Prophet pursues more clearly in another place, saying: *If (a watchman) see the sword coming upon the land and sound the trumpet and tell the people, then he that heareth the sound of the trumpet, whosoever he be, and doth not look to himself, if the sword come and cut him off, his blood shall be upon his own head. He heard the sound of the trumpet and did not look to himself; his blood shall be on him. But if he look to himself, he shall save his life."* ·Here, moreover, the Word of God shows what he who performs the office of watchman should do: namely, when he sees the sword coming upon the land— the wrath of God, that is, upon sinners who are given over to earthly works—he should under no circumstances be silent; and as long as they cling to their sins, he should not cease to declare that the punishment of the divine displeasure awaits them; indeed, he should rebuke them loudly and publicly— for this the word trumpet implies—that so by cleansing themselves from their sins they may escape the punishment of future damnation. If, however, worldly men contemn him who reproves them and makes known the future wrath which already threatens its despisers, their blood is upon themselves; and it is impossible that the priest who did not pass over their sins in silence should share the punishment that awaits them.

CHAPTER 23

*Priests, including those who can do otherwise, should teach
so simply that all may understand what they teach.*

" And certainly a bishop will not excuse himself on the
plea of ignorance, as though he cannot teach because his
speech is not adequate and clear; for a priest's doctrine should
be none other than his life, and those who listen can profit
enough if they hear their teachers teach even with simplicity
what they see them perform in a spiritual manner, as the
Apostle says: *Although . . . rude in speech, yet not in
knowledge.*[78] From this it may be understood that a teacher
of the Church should not parade an elaborate style, lest he
seem not to want to edify the Church of God but to reveal
what great learning he possesses.[79] Not in the glitter of his
words, then, but in the virtue of his deeds let him place all
his confidence in preaching. Let him delight not in the
shouts of the people who acclaim him but in their tears. Let
him be zealous to desire not applause [80] from the people but
their sighs. That especially let the teacher of the Church
elaborate which may make his hearers better men by reason
of sound discussions, not applauders through vain flattery.
The tears which he desires his listeners to shed let him first
weep himself and so inflame them by the contrition of his
own heart. Such should be the simplicity and straightfor-
wardness of the bishop's language: though this may mean less
good Latin,[81] it should be restrained and dignified so that it
prevents no one, however ignorant, from understanding it but
sinks with a certain charm into the heart of all who hear it.

CHAPTER 24

*The difference between teachers who edify the Church by
teaching simply and those who vaunt their own
eloquence by brilliant oratory.*

" In fine, the purpose of rhetoricians is one thing, and
that of teachers should be another. The former with all the
force of their eloquence aspire to the display of studied declamation; the latter by moderate and ordinary language seek the
glory of Christ. The former clothe empty subject matter
with extravagant verbal ornamentation; the latter adorn and
grace simple words with true ideas. Rhetoricians endeavor
to hide the ugliness of their thoughts by a veil, as it were,
of fine language; [82] teachers try to give grace to the inelegance
of their statements by means of precious thoughts. The
former put all their glory in the favor of the people; the latter,
in the assistance of God. The former speak in a manner
worthy of applause and avail their hearers nothing; the latter
teach in ordinary language and instruct their imitators because they do not vitiate their doctrine by any affectation of
an ornate style.

CHAPTER 25

*Characteristics of priests who wish to become sharers in
the contemplative life.*

1. " Therefore, if holy priests—not such as the divine
threat declares are to be sentenced and condemned,[83] but
such as the apostolic teaching commends [84]—convert many to
God by their holy living and preaching; if they display no
imperiousness, but do everything humbly and show them-

selves through love of holy charity affable to those over whom they have been placed; if they in some cases cure the weaknesses of their carnally living brethren by the medicine of healing words and in others bear patiently with those whom they judge to be incurable; if in the lives they live and in their preaching they seek not their own glory but Christ's; if they do not woefully waste either their words or their deeds as the price of courting favor, but always ascribe to God whatever honor is paid them as they live and teach in a priestly manner; if the dutiful greetings of those they meet do not make them proud but weigh them down; if they consider themselves not honored but burdened by the praises of those who compliment them; [85] if they console the afflicted, feed the needy, clothe the naked, redeem the captives, harbor strangers; if they show wanderers the way of salvation and promise hope to those who despair of gaining pardon; if they spur on those who make progress, and arouse those who are delaying, and are constantly occupied with whatever pertains to their office: who will be such a stranger to faith as to doubt that such men are sharers in the contemplative virtue, by whose words as well as example many become coheirs of the kingdom of heaven? [86]

2. " These are the ministers of the word,[87] helpers of God, oracles of the Holy Spirit. Through such men God is reconciled with His people; the people are instructed unto God. These are the successors of the Lord's Apostles, who, wondrously endowed with apostolic virtues, rule the churches which the former established by sublime miracles; who defend the Catholic faith by preaching, or if necessity demands, by the rending of their limbs. To maintain the faith in all its strength they are prepared to lose their possessions and

even to die. They grow with the virtues of faithful Catholics who make progress through them, God being the cause; and, clinging inseparably to their God, in whom they are confident that their true and lasting goods are stored, they spurn the fleeting joys of this world."

Thus far have I prolonged my talk, with the fullness of detailed discussion, on three topics: here I have, I think, adequately shown the nature of the contemplative life, the difference there is between it and the active life, and how priests can become sharers in the contemplative virtue. Therefore, at length bringing this book to a close, I shall, God helping my effort because of your prayers, treat three further questions in the second book; thus in the third book I can deal with the four remaining topics, which involve the doctrine of the vices and virtues to be discussed.

BOOK TWO

1. Having presented in the preceding book the norm of the contemplative life, I have set myself the task, according to the strength the Lord will grant me, to treat the active life as I promised. Wherefore, as I did in the preface to the first book, here, too, I shall in a few words make known the obligation imposed on me to write; for, if I could without impairment of obedience have refused what you commanded, never by the impulse of my own will would I give myself over to be attacked by the malevolent tooth of critics who, refusing to consider how reluctantly I undertook to write this, will perhaps attribute it all—what is wholly your bidding —to the vice of vanity; and this all the more if, in speaking of matters wherein the way of life incumbent upon practically all ecclesiastics is described, I should write of anything that might offend the minds of those who live in a worldly manner; and because they would see in the description of the ecclesiastical life their own conduct made public—something which they wish to be unknown rather than corrected —in their carnal-mindedness they would be aroused and would rage against me as the betrayer of their deeds; and though they would judge that what I had brought out with the help of God was judiciously said, they would, nevertheless, argue that I should not have said it; and so they would mock at either the subject of the discussion or the person

treating it. But because a sensible mind should seek the fruit of obedience incomparably more than avoid the opprobrium of unjust blame, I believed the judgment of those who would find fault with my words to be a more tolerable burden than the danger of obstinate disobedience. Confident, then, that you, who commanded me to discuss this, will beg and gain for me from the Lord the power of finishing my task and will excuse my presumption among those who are going to criticize me, I shall despatch the work I have begun, aided by your prayers.

2. But before I take up in detail each of the questions you proposed, I think I should make a few general remarks about the matter to be discussed in this little book. Thus it will become evident why I said in advance that I could be criticized by those who pay more attention to who says a thing than to what he says; who investigate with distorted examination not the reasoning of the statements but the rank of those who utter them, and flinch from having mentioned to them that which they do not wish to do or become. They prefer to remain ignorant of a point of doctrine, even one they are eager to know, rather than to learn it from a person of inferior rank, although truth, from whatever source it becomes manifest, is to be attributed not to human proficiency but to God; and they should believe truth not merely when coming from certain sources but from all—truth, which is of itself such that it does not first become great when great men teach it; no, truth itself makes great those who have the capacity of teaching it or learning it.

Now, you wished the nature of the active life explained to you for this reason: that you might prove that you and your followers always have lived and are living in accordance with it, not that you might learn from my discussion how to live. The religious way of life is really the active life, which teaches how superiors should rule and love those under them, and, being not less careful of the salvation of their charges than of their own, should with paternal care provide what they know is advantageous for them; and how subjects should serve their superior as members of the body serve the head,[1] and with great love should carry out his orders as the will of God, judging that to be holy, profitable, and necessary for them which has pleased their superior, not that which the pride of a corrupt mind has dictated to them for their destruction. And for that reason, being grounded in the virtue of obedience and patience, they do not discuss the orders of their superiors but fulfill them; and when strictness of discipline requires that they be severely reproved, they bear magnanimously the correction they have received and ascribe their chastisement not to the passions of those who rebuke them but to their own negligences.

How priests also should treat and rule their subjects—commoners and nobles, the rich and the powerful—the sequel of this book will contain. As I have already said repeatedly, I would not venture to write these things if I could have refused you anything. But now let me set down the questions to be discussed. You asked, then, whether those who contemn the divine commands should receive calm toleration or should be reproved in proportion to their sins with ecclesiastical severity.

TABLE OF CONTENTS

An objection: Why do holy priests whose care it is to reprove those who live wickedly, bear religious pretenders calmly? 5. In reply: Certain considerations may require the gentle treatment of the faults of some. 6. Those who do not think on their own sins show no patience in reproaching others. 7. The remedial value of confessing one's sins; the punishment incurred by deceitful concealment of sins. 8. Those who reprove unjustly and insincerely are liars and will be condemned by the divine judgment.

9. Priests should have nothing of their own and should receive the possessions of the Church as common goods of which they are to render an account to God. 10. The harm done to their soul by those who, having enough of their own, take anything from the Church, which feeds the poor. 11. The case of those who even with profit to their soul are supported by the resources of the Church. 12. The obligation of those clerics who are too weak to renounce their possessions. 13. True joys and true riches; the goods of this life are but an impediment to lovers of the blessings to come. 14. The interpretation of the Apostle's statement: *They who work in the holy place eat the things that are of the holy place.* 15. Covetousness and its domination of those of whom it has once taken possession. 16. Those possess God more perfectly who renounce earthly possessions from their hearts.

17. Those profit nothing who though abstaining from food are slaves to their vices; nor does it avail those who do their own will to renounce their possessions. 18. The first man lost great blessings by his disregard of abstinence. 19. The sin of the first man and the evils which followed his sin by the judgment of God. 20. Having been restored in Christ, we

shall regain all the blessings which we lost when corrupted in Adam. 21. The life incumbent upon those who desire to imitate Christ. 22. The practice of temperance in those who desire to abstain from the pleasure of delicacies or from an immoderate eating of common foods and from an immoderate use of wine. 23. The desire of meats, not their nature, defiles those who use meats. 24. It is often beneficial to place hospitality shown to visitors before fasting or abstinence.

CHAPTER 1

According to the different kinds of sinners some are to be tolerated, others are to be censured.

If all together suffered from the very same trouble of mind and, being afflicted with identical disorders of the soul, did not differ from one another, it would be necessary to tolerate all or to reprove all. But as it is, some are to be borne with, others are to be chastised [2] because according to the difference in sinners the type of prescription also differs. And, surely, different remedies are to be applied to sins [3] just as the sins themselves arise from different causes. For the habit of sin entices many; others the opportunity for some temporal gain allures to sin; frailty inclines some; ignorance of the good causes some not to know that they are sinning, and, though they are reproached, the fascination that evil holds for them prevents them from ever learning what they do not know. I do not mention those who are stained by the sins of others to which they consent. I also omit those who, desiring to attain what they love or refusing to suffer what they fear, either betray the Catholic faith or barter away the excellence of truth for falsehood. But this I do say: who does not know that men sin in one way by unpremeditated thought, in another by determination; in one way by speech, in another by deed; in one way by necessity, in another of their own will?

2. Since, then, men sin in so many and such very different ways, who does not understand that those whose maladies are so varied certainly cannot be cured by one and the same method? Besides, human frailty spurns God's precepts in two ways: either by doing what He has forbidden or by not doing what He has ordered. But since those who do not perform His commands contemn Him in His precepts not only for the reasons I have stated but also for others I have not mentioned, so they all should be cured, now by teaching, now by exhortation, now by tolerance, now by rebuke, so that with Christ's help the salvation of no one in this life should be despaired of.

Now, then, if I have made it sufficiently clear that we should use both forbearance and reprimand in dealing with those who spurn the divine commands, I ought to show, while you help me through your merits and prayers, by whom, how, in what order, and how long those who are being cured should be cared for.

CHAPTER 2

In praise of holy priests.

1. And lest my discussion, as expressing human opinion, fail to commend itself to belief and lose its effect by being trusted too little, I shall try to show by divine testimony that those things are true which I have proposed to prove with the help of the Lord. Let me first, however, bring out a few

points in praise of true priests who are the heads of churches. They especially have received the charge of caring for souls. Ably bearing the responsibility for the people entrusted to them, they untiringly supplicate God for the sins of all as for their own; and, like an Aaron,[4] offering the sacrifice of a contrite heart and a humble spirit,[4a] which appeases God, they turn the wrath of future punishment from their people. By the grace of God they become indicators of the divine will, founders of the churches of Christ after the Apostles, leaders of the faithful, champions of truth, enemies of perverse teaching, amiable to all the good, terrifying even in appearance to those of evil conscience, avengers of the oppressed, fathers of those regenerated in the Catholic faith, preachers of the things of heaven, shock troops in battles unseen, patterns of good works, examples of virtues, and models for the faithful. They are the glory of the Church, in whom her lustre is enhanced; they are the very strong pillars [5] which, founded on Christ, support the whole multitude of believers; they are the gates of the eternal city through which all who believe in Christ enter unto Him; they are the gatekeepers who have received the keys of the kingdom of heaven; they are also the stewards of the royal house whose decision assigns each one's rank and office in the court of the eternal King.

2. These are they who have merited the priesthood not by courting favor but by living spiritually; who, elevated not by the support of human patronage but by divine approbation, do not applaud themselves because of the excellence of their high office; who do not hold their heads high because of the honor they have received but are occupied with the labor imposed; who on being advanced think not of their pre-

5 ‘

eminence but of their weight of cares; who do not glory in
the dignity of their office but rather labor under their burden
when appointed. Such men Holy Scripture calls " watch-
men," [6] men who watch over everyone's acts and examine
with the application of a holy curiosity how each one lives
at home with his family and in the community with his
fellow citizens. Those with whom they are satisfied they
encourage by honoring them; those whom they find wicked
they correct by reproving them; and if they are not willing
to be corrected, they bear it calmly since they will gain fruit
in abundance either because of their strictness if those whom
they chided have improved, or because of their patience, not-
withstanding that those with whom they show forbearance
have not accepted correction.

CHAPTER 3

The apostolic testimony and its exposition.

1. But now let me cite the divine proofs as I promised.
In the Acts of the Apostles the Apostle Paul says: *Behold, I
know that all you among whom I have walked, preaching
the kingdom of Jesus Christ, shall see my face no more.
Wherefore, I take you to witness this day that I am clear
from the blood of all men; for I have not spared to declare
unto you all the counsel of God. Take heed to yourselves
and to the whole flock wherein the Holy Ghost hath placed
you bishops to rule the Church of God, which He hath purchased with His own blood.*[7] "The kingdom of God," he
says, "I have preached, walking among you, that I might
keep myself free from the damnation of all those who, after
hearing the word of the saving doctrine, are not moved to

salvation." He preaches the kingdom of God [8] who does not cease to preach of the future life, which has no end; of divine contemplation, which has no palling weariness; of the happiness of the saints, which does not fail; of gaining the likeness of angels: [9] so that if his listeners have not been willing to be drawn to these ineffable blessings, he who preached to them and was not silent is not to blame.

2. But as to what he adds in the following: *For I have not spared to declare unto you all the counsel of God,*[10] what else does he mean to be understood except that the teacher of the Church reveals the direction of God—and this the Apostle calls "the counsel of God"—to those whom he teaches? Now, he reveals the plan of the divine direction when he teaches that fathers by showing love to their children should merit it from the Lord, who is the Father of all; that children should show due honor to their fathers, not constrained by the fear of being disinherited, but prompted by the desire of future reward. For fathers by loving their children, as much as children by showing honor to their fathers, fulfill the command of the Lord, who ordered both these things to be done. He teaches that husbands should preserve the fidelity of the marriage bed with their wives; that wives should please their husbands not by the care given to alluring beauty or by the exquisiteness of their dress, but by the gravity of their morals and the holiness of their acts; that masters should treat their slaves mercifully,[11] showing themselves their brother servants in Christ,[12] and that slaves should so obey their masters from their hearts that they accomplish the will not only of their masters but also of God, who commands this; [13] that citizens should maintain true peace with their fellow citizens, friends with friends, parents

with children; that in business no one should deceive another by crafty fraud or in a mutual agreement break the faith which the other party wishes to be kept.

3. Through these and similar statements the priest by preaching announces, and the people by obeying receive God's counsel, without which no one reaches the kingdom wherein only such as carry out the divine counsel will by God's plan share in celestial rewards. Then, as to the Apostle's statement: *Take heed to yourselves and to the whole flock wherein the Holy Ghost hath placed you bishops to rule the Church of God, which He hath purchased with His own blood,*[14] who does not see that then do priests take heed to themselves when by living holy lives and by preaching faithfully the will of the Lord they take heed to the Church of God, so that it is not difficult for them to bear with the weak ones of the Church [15] for whose redemption the Author of life deigned to give Himself over to death? But let those who are taught show understanding; let those who are rebuked manifest at least some progress for the reprimand they have received; let those who are treated with forbearance finally feel ashamed of their grave sins and by profiting from their correction give joy to their teacher, through whose patience they are gently treated; let them, I say, cheerfully hear what God's word commands them by the mouth of the Apostle: *Obey*, he says, *your prelates and be subject to them; for they watch as being to render an account of your souls; that they may do this with joy and not with grief. For this is expedient for you.*[16]

4. Therefore, those who hear should obey their teachers and be subject to them with reverence. They do this who, when given a reproof, accept it willingly and do not oppose

those who rebuke them. But as to what he says: *For they watch as being to render an account of your souls*, he clearly shows concern for the people entrusted to him who, watchful in his conduct as well as in his preaching, carefully searches out the snares of the ancient enemy lest the devil by subtle cunning steal anyone, like a wolf while the shepherd sleeps, and bring him with himself to eternal torture, snatching him away unto the shepherd's loss. But because among those who are chastised some correct themselves obediently while others continue to the end in their perversity, on that account he says of priests: *that they may do this with joy and not with grief*. Priests rebuke with joy when those they reprove draw profit; and they rebuke with grief when they sorrow that they accomplish nothing in those who ignore them. And thus, he says that it is *expedient* for the faithful that priests reproach *with joy and not with grief*; that the faithful give joy to their teachers by their correction and increase their happiness by their progress.

CHAPTER 4

An objection: Why do holy priests whose care it is to reprove those who live wickedly, bear religious pretenders calmly?

1. I had not yet completed my discussion about holy priests, on which subject I was venturing to say more, when one of our friends came in and curiously asked me what I was dictating. After I had it read to him, he said: "There is no doubt that all bishops ought to be such as your discussion has set forth and that in our day there are many among us full of priestly good qualities as you have truthfully

said; but with this established that it pertains to their office to correct the unruly with priestly authority, to teach the ignorant, to refute those who attack sound doctrine, why is it that they do not extend this attention of theirs to all? Why do they not reprove others, too, with the same force? I mean those who, pretending to be converted, cast off nothing of their former ways, being changed not in their hearts but only in their dress, not in fact but only in appearance.

2. " These are the people who, content to have renounced the world in word only, not in deed, live in a worldly manner and hide their faults under the empty profession of a better life and, cloaked by the name of pretended religion, assume a reputation for virtue instead of true virtue. They preach great things but do not perform them; they attack vices but do not lay aside their own. In public they pretend to be displeased with what they do in secret; they are eager to seem great, not to become great; they praise those by whose commendation they desire to be praised; they fast that they may sell the pallor of their face for noxious esteem. Prompt to censure others, they do not allow anyone to criticize them even slightly. For the sake of public appearance they pretend patience, but in their mind they hide carefully the poison of wrath,[17] ready to harm when they find an opportunity to harm; unconcerned over their own deeds, they become censors of others with insolent liberty. They impudently foist themselves upon holy virgins and widows and are smitten with so much affection for them that they would more readily withdraw from communion with the Church—a wicked thing even to say—than from their company. Although perhaps they do not sin with them, yet, by furnishing matter for evil suspicion, they stain their life with the stigma of a bad reputation.

3. "I pass over those persons who, with an undulating motion of their unsteady body, step along with their garments flowing to their ankles, and moving wave-like, as it were, in the wanton flexings of their hips, betray the dissoluteness of their souls in steps that sway with sinuous movement. Who can bear with those who, affecting shammed honesty, undertake the cause of orphans and widows with feigned piety as though to protect them? [18] Their motive is to add the possessions of such to their own and, becoming rich from being poor, or richer from being rich, wickedly to build up their slender resources: the day when they will live more sumptuously by reason of their bulging possessions, they must never lack material for the pleasures of their gluttonous appetites. Why, then, do not those who have divinely received the power to censure reprove such persons? Do they not fear that perhaps, by sparing those who live in such a manner, they appear to approve their deeds? What of the fact that they even admit them to the clerical office and—O shame— as though it were not enough that they leave severity alone and do not censure such men, even honor them besides?"

CHAPTER 5

In reply: Certain considerations may require the gentle treatment of the faults of some.

1. But I replied: "If you recall what I have said of holy priests, you have been adequately answered; for the teachers of the Church, as I have already said above, should possess both the faculty of censure in order to chastise and patience in order to tolerate with fortitude those who are unwilling to be corrected. Thus they obey the command of the Apostle,

who instructed Timothy, saying: *Reprove, entreat, rebuke in all patience and doctrine,*[19] as though he would say: " Reprove your equals; entreat your elders; rebuke your juniors." But he added *in all patience and doctrine* because the man gently reprimanded shows reverence for his reprover, while one who is offended by the harshness of immoderate correction accepts neither the reproof nor salvation. So, too, in another place the same Apostle says: *You who are stronger, bear the infirmities of the weaker.*[20] Therefore, they calmly tolerate as sick those whom they cannot correct by reproof. Accordingly, because it is not expedient to rebuke all severely or to treat all gently, holy priests know and distinguish between those whom they should reprove with moderate severity and those whom they should tolerate with priestly magnanimity; and thus they have regard not for the wishes but for the advantage of all for whom they provide by God's grace. Besides, they forbear to honor some who seek honor unduly, for whom they know it is not advantageous, not through the vice of any envy but through a counsel of deep prudence; and they honor others who desire to be hidden, so that they may open a way for them to greater advancement. They chastise those of whom they know that they can bear rebuke; and they feel their way with those who cannot bear reproof, as being weak, not by flattering them because they are such but by compassionating the infirmities of such persons if it happens that they cannot be healed otherwise.

2. " But if the weak who cannot be cured by the application of reproof are debarred from communion with the Church, being burdened beyond measure by the weight of intolerable sadness, they either break down and shun the sight of all holy persons through whom they could be restored

to God, or are certain to leap into every shameless sin if they are embittered; and they will do in public the evil they used to do in secret. They fall into so great madness through despair of regaining salvation that with insolent wit they turn the serious words of their reprovers into evil jests; and, turning upon themselves with deadly cynicism,[21] they boast of their own baseness, and thus feast the evil joys of the wicked. On this account, then, those who cannot be reproved because of their weakness are to be tolerated with gentle compassion. And, truly, if you produce a healthy sense of shame in a sinner because you blush for him and if by the tender compassion of your heart you transfer to him the shame which you assume for his sins, you will easily repress in him all laxity with regard to sin and take from him all the overbearance which incites to wanton baseness. Then modesty, guardian of integrity, will adorn his behavior so that what formerly seemed despicable to him when he was despicable pleases him, and that seems despicable to him which formerly pleased him when he was displeasing to all the good. He will follow holy men by loving them; and by following them he will fashion himself gradually to their likeness by correcting his previous way of life, with the result that, as laborious as it was for him to climb to the summit of virtue, so base would it be to him to descend again to the vices he rejoices to have abandoned. For, just as virtue is oppressive to the wicked, so vicious pleasure is bitter to the friend of virtue. There you see how one who thinks of nothing but the salvation of those he wishes to help treats all sinners gently, or rebukes them."

CHAPTER 6

Those who do not think on their own sins show no patience in reproaching others.

It is a fact that a man is ignorant of his own sins, which he ought to acknowledge and mourn, as long as he pries and probes into those of others. But if, turning to himself, he looks to his own morals, he seeks not what he may especially blame in others but what he may grieve for in himself. We should, then, not be prompt to rebuke the faults of our brethren but sorrow over them so that, carrying our burdens for one another, we can fulfill the law of Christ,[22] who surely did not chide our sins but who bore them as the Evangelist says: *Behold the Lamb of God, behold Him who taketh away the sins of the world.*[23] Therefore, if He who was without any sin whatsoever suffered us sinners with ineffable affection and does not cease to suffer us, desiring not our death but our improvement—not the death of sinners but their salvation [24]—why should not we, after the example of our Savior and Lord, bear with the weak, seeing that we ourselves are weak and wish God to bear with us, or, should we be strong, can yet become weak, being frail?

CHAPTER 7

The remedial value of confessing one's sins; the punishment incurred by deceitful concealment of sins.

Furthermore, sins themselves are so hidden—those of others from us and our own from them—that very often a saint is concealed among sinners, and a sinner attains the reputation of a saint. When an innocent man cannot protect himself, the rash suspicion of a judge condemns him, while the cleverness of an alert talent clears a guilty man; but of course in such cases not the divine judgment but the human is deceived. And is it remarkable that we do not know without their own confession what the souls of others are, since we so know even ourselves today as not to know what we are going to be tomorrow? But when any of our brethren reveal to us the sins which oppress them, as they show physicians the wounds troubling them, we should endeavor with the help of God to heal them as quickly as possible to prevent their growing worse because of the lack of attention. And as to the sins of any persons that somehow come to light though in their guilt they did not intend to confess them, whatever sins are not remedied by the gentle medication of patience are to be cauterized and cured by the fire, as it were, of kindly reproof.

2. But if even the remedy of such gentle forbearance and kindly reprimand avails nothing in persons who, though long endured and admonished for their own good, refuse to amend, like decaying parts of the body they should be cut off by the knife of excommunication.[25] Otherwise, just as morbid flesh, if not removed, impairs the health of the rest of the body by the infection it brings, so those who despise correction and persist in their infirmity, by remaining with their depraved morals in the company of the good people, will infect them by the example of their own wickedness. But those whose sins escape human notice, being neither self-confessed nor exposed by others, if they have been unwilling to confess them and amend, will have God, whom they have as their witness, as their avenger also.[26] And what do they

profit in escaping human judgment when, if they persist in their evil, they will go by God's punishment into eternal torture? If, however, they become their own judges and, as though avengers of their own iniquity, here exercise the voluntary penalty of a most severe punishment against themselves, they will exchange eternal torments for temporal; and with their tears flowing from true contrition of heart they will extinguish the flames of the everlasting fire. But those who, established in any clerical rank, commit grave sin in secret deceive themselves by empty persuasion if they think they ought to receive Communion and discharge their office because they escape the notice of men by hiding their sin.

3. For, apart from those sins which are so slight that they cannot be avoided and for the expiation of which we call upon God daily, saying: *Forgive us our debts as we also forgive our debtors*,[27] we must avoid those grave sins which, when published, cause those who commit them to be condemned by human judgment. Those, however, who commit them and fear to confess them lest they receive the just penalty of excommunication, communicate without good reason; nay, truly, they heap up the wrath of the divine indignation doubly against themselves, both because they pretend innocence to men and because, contemning God's judgment, they are ashamed to abstain from the altar through human respect. Therefore, those will more easily reconcile God who acknowledge their sin, not convicted by human judgment, but of their own accord; [28] who either reveal it by their own confession or who, if others do not know what they are in secret, bring sentence of voluntary excommunication against themselves; [29] and, separating themselves not in heart but in duties from the altar which they ministered, mourn for their

life as though it were dead, being sure that when God has been reconciled to them by the fruits of efficacious penance they not only will recover what they have lost but will also be made citizens of the eternal city and receive everlasting joys.

CHAPTER 8

Those who reprove unjustly and insincerely are liars and will be condemned by the divine judgment.

Now, it is not for me to say anything of those who, prompted by slight suspicion, rebuke men who live uprightly so that they confuse and discourage them through ungrounded correction and thereby seek for themselves the glory of an ill-considered severity. Of these God's word speaks so clearly that it does not need an expositor; for the Holy Spirit says in Ecclesiasticus: *There is a lying rebuke in the anger of an insolent man; and there is a judgment that is not good.*[30] Indeed, the rebuke of an insolent and domineering man, which here is called " lying," is the judgment of pride and not of any humility, and therefore is not good. What could be said more plainly, more patently, than to say that he who rebukes falsely is " insolent "? For he who reproves falsely is insolent; and he who is insolent reproves falsely. Likewise, He says in Proverbs: *A false witness shall not be unpunished; and he that speaketh lies shall not escape.*[31] Who is a false witness if not he who accuses any man of crimes without due inquiry? He says that one who rebukes unjustly *shall not be unpunished* for this reason that, by reproving when no faults demand censure, he wishes the innocent to seem guilty. But when He says of the man who rebukes unjustly that he *shall not escape*, what else is to be understood except that he who reproves anyone, not to correct him, but to vaunt himself insultingly, will not escape the anger of God?

But let what I have said suffice concerning those who despise God's precepts and concerning the virtue of correction and patience. I must not, by dwelling too long on one question, touch upon the rest too briefly, nor tax your attention by the length of an immoderately extensive volume. Let us see, then, what the contents of the next chapter teach us further: whether, so it reads, it is expedient to hold the goods of the Church to provide for the community life of the brethren and their support,[32] or to spurn them through love of perfection.

CHAPTER 9

Priests should have nothing of their own and should receive the possessions of the Church as common goods of which they are to render an account to God.

1. It is expedient to hold the goods of the Church and to despise one's own possessions through love of perfection. For the wealth of the Church is not one's own, but common; and, therefore, whoever has given away or sold all that he owns and has become a despiser of his own property, when he has been put in charge of a church, becomes steward of all the church possesses. Thus the saintly Paulinus,[33] as you yourself know better than I, sold the immense estates he had and distributed the proceeds to the poor. But when afterwards he had become bishop, he did not contemn the property of his church but administered it most faithfully. By doing this he showed sufficiently both that one's own posses-

sions should be despised for the sake of perfection and that those things which are common property of the Church can be possessed without harm to perfection. What did the saintly Hilary do? [34] Did not he also leave all his goods to his parents or sell them and distribute the proceeds to the poor? Yet, when because of his perfection he became bishop of the church of Arles, he not only held what that church owned at the time but also increased it by accepting numerous legacies from the faithful. These most holy and perfect bishops, then, show by plain deeds that what they did can and should be done. Surely, these men, most certainly learned in secular as well as divine studies, who had given up all their own property, would never have kept the property of the Church if they had known that it should be despised.

2. The conclusion is that such great men who, wishing to become followers of Christ, renounced all they had, held the property of the Church not as owners but as stewards. And, therefore, knowing that the possessions of the Church are but the vows[35] of the faithful, the ransom of sinners, and the patrimony of the poor, they did not claim them for their own use, as being their own, but divided them as a trust among the poor. For this is to despise things while possessing them—to hold them not for oneself but for others, not to seek property for the church because of a lust to possess but to accept it because of the sacred obligation to aid the needy. What the Church owns she has in common with all those who have nothing; and she should not give anything of it to those who have enough of their own, since to give anything to those who have is only to squander it.

CHAPTER 10

The harm done to their soul by those who, having enough
of their own, take anything from the Church,
which feeds the poor.

1. Further, those who, though having possessions of their
own, desire to be given something do not take without griev-
ous sin that wherefrom a poor man was to receive his living.
It is evidently of clerics that the Holy Spirit says: *They*
eat the sins of my people.[36] Now, here those who have nothing of their own take not sin but the sustenance they evidently lack; conversely, those who have possessions take not
the sustenance in which they abound but the sins of others.
Even the poor, if they can help themselves by their crafts
and labors, should not usurp what the weak and the sick
ought to receive, lest the Church in her capacity of furnishing
the necessities of life to those destitute of every comfort be
embarrassed by the fact that even such as are in no need at
all are recipients of her aid and be unable to assist those
she should.

2. They, moreover, who serve the Church and, believing
that they should receive a return for their labor as their due,
either accept readily or demand what they do not need, are
too carnal-minded if they think that those who serve the
Church faithfully receive earthly pay and not rather eternal
rewards. It is but natural that in the world the profession of
arms, having no heavenly recompenses to give, pays out
earthly ones to those who fight valiantly; hence, it certainly
is a shame if the faithful and laborious devotion of clerics
renounces eternal rewards for temporal pay. If, however, a
minister of the Church does not have the wherewithal of

life, let not the Church give him his recompense here, but let her furnish him the necessities of life. Thus he will receive the reward of his labor in the future—a reward to which he looks forward, established in the hope of the Lord's promise. Again, as to those who, ostensibly self-sufficient, do not ask that anything be given them as their due, but yet live at the expense of the Church, it is not for me to say with what kind of sin they presume to take the food of the poor. By what they pay out to themselves they only put an additional burden upon the Church, which they should have aided with their own resources; hence, you will perhaps find them living in community so as not to feed any of the poor or take in strangers or cause a reduction of their own wealth through every-day expenditures. But if they do give any of their income to the Church in return for their own support, they must not by silly bragging make display of themselves before the indigent whom the Church feeds and clothes; for one who strips himself of the things of the world, or one who, having nothing, desires nothing, is more perfect than he who of his many possessions gives something to the Church and perhaps boasts of what he has given.

3. The things I say are severe, and I do not deny it. Severe they are, but only to such as are unwilling to observe them. Yet, if these things are done: difficult as they are to those who do not do them, they immediately become easy when they do them. Hence, it is not the impossibility of doing them, but their strangeness, that makes difficult the things we are unwilling to perform; let them become a habit, and, done again and again, they cause no one trouble. After all, I ask you, which of the things I have mentioned is difficult? That a man should not take from the Church what he does not need? Or that he should renounce that which he

possesses without cogent reason? If he does not wish to abandon his possessions on this account that he may have wherewith to live, why does he take that for which he will be accountable? Why does he go elsewhere to multiply the sins he commits with his own possessions?

CHAPTER 11

The case of those who even with profit to their soul are supported by the resources of the Church.

Accordingly, the priest to whom the office of administration has been entrusted will receive from the people, not only without cupidity but also with a reputation for conscientiousness, things to be distributed; and he will dispense them faithfully—he who has either left that which was his own to his kinsfolk or distributed it to the poor or added it to the property of the Church, and placed himself for the love of poverty in the number of the poor, so that he himself lives as one voluntarily poor on what he administers to the poor. Clerics, too, poor either by choice or by birth, whether living in homes of their own or in community houses, can receive with fullness of virtue the necessities of life because greed of possessing does not lead them to accept them, but the necessity of living forces them.

CHAPTER 12

The obligation of those clerics who are too weak to renounce their possessions.

Those, however, who are so weak that they cannot renounce their possessions, if they leave the things they were going to receive to a steward to be given to the indigent, keep their own property without sin because in a certain manner they, too, give up their possessions when, being content with their own, they take nothing of what they think is due their labor or their rank. But if they think that they should receive a portion of those things that are given to the Church for this reason that they may not appear to throw it away, and if they think that they cannot abandon their possessions because it is improper for them to be reduced to poverty in the midst of their families, let them realize that it is an abomination for people of means to be fed with the alms of the poor.

CHAPTER 13

True joys and true riches; the goods of this life are but an impediment to lovers of the blessings to come.

1. Alas, how subtly the master of deceit ensnares us, with what blindness he veils the eyes of our mind lest, eager for joy, we discover a truer source of joy, or, desiring to grow in riches, learn what riches we should incomparably prefer. For it is indeed good to rejoice; but if the one who rejoices does not rejoice for the reason he should, his joy cannot be good. For the thief, too, rejoices when he has stolen what he wants; the drunkard, when he has found opportunity for a desired debauch; the adulterer, when he attains the pleasure of enjoying the body for which he lusts. But although it is a good thing to rejoice, it is a great evil to rejoice in these and similar things, in which the world, which will perish with its lovers, wishes us to rejoice. These are the things we should spurn so that we may rejoice ineffably in a good conscience,

in holiness of morals, in the increase of virtues, in the gift of God, and in the promise of the future kingdom.

2. To acquire wealth is also a great good; but to grow rich from a source whence you should not is not an advantage to be desired but a calamity to be shunned. For there is no one more unfortunate and no one more miserable than he who prospers by unjust gains, whom frauds and thefts enrich. Those riches we ought to seek which can both adorn and protect us, which we cannot acquire or lose against our will; which arm us against the attacks of the enemy, separate us from the world, commend us to God, enrich and ennoble our souls; which dwell with us and within us. These are to be considered our wealth: modesty, which makes us modest; justice, which makes us just; piety, which makes us pious; humility, which makes us humble; gentleness, which makes us gentle; innocence, which makes us innocent; purity, which makes us pure; prudence, which makes us prudent; temperance, which makes us temperate; and love, which makes us dear to God and men, powerful in virtues, despisers of the world, and pursuers of all good.[37] These are the holy virtues not of all but of the holy; the possessions not of the proud rich but of the humble poor; the patrimony of hearts, the incorruptible riches of good morals, in which only those abound who renounce carnal riches from their hearts. Although these latter are also good since they have been created by a good God, yet, because they are common to the good and the wicked, spiritual men strive to renounce them so that they can attain to those incomparably better things which are the property of all good persons; for the good which even the wicked possess is not so excellent a good as that which only the good possess.

3. When the unjust possess a bodily good, it is their reward; when the just possess it, it is not their recompense but a temporal consolation. Thus, the loss of a temporal good becomes a trial to the just, a punishment to the unjust; for the just man, captivated by a desire for heavenly things, does not at all feel it whether he possesses all temporal things or loses them, while the wicked man does not lose without sorrow what he possesses with delight. Consequently, those who fight for God should with all their hearts shun riches, which those who desire to possess do not seek without labor, do not find without difficulty, do not preserve without care, do not possess without anxious effort, do not lose without grief. Moreover, the Apostle says to the soldiers of Christ: *I would have you to be without solicitude;* [38] and, *The desire of money is the root of all evils, which some coveting have erred from the faith and have entangled themselves in many sorrows.* [39] And so, earthly wealth is, for those who love it wickedly, material not for pleasures but for sorrows; wherefore, it is expedient that the property of the Church be possessed to provide support for those who serve not the world, whose fleeting joys they spurn, but God, whose ineffable blessings they desire.

CHAPTER 14

The interpretation of the Apostle's statement: They who work in the holy place eat the things that are of the holy place.

Of such men, it appears, the Apostle says: *They who work in the holy place eat the things that are of the holy place; and they that serve the altar partake with the altar.* [40] If he did not intend this to be understood of those who renounce their own possessions, he certainly would not have followed this up with: *So also God ordained that they who preach the Gospel should live by the Gospel.*[41] They live by the Gospel who wish to have nothing of their own, who neither have nor desire to have anything, possessing not their own things but things in common. What does it mean " to live by the Gospel " except that the laborer should receive the necessaries of life there where he works? Nevertheless, the Apostle, who so preached the Gospel that he did not live by the Gospel but furnished his necessities by his own hands, boldly says of himself: *But I have used none of these things.*[42] And why he said this he revealed, continuing: *for it is good for me to die rather than that any man should make my glory void.*[43] He says that his glory would have been made void if he had wished to receive his subsistence from those to whom he preached; for he wished to receive the reward of his labor not in this life but in the future life. But if he who had nothing wished to live not by the Gospel wherein he labored but by his own hands lest he lose the glory of his reward, what of us who do not wish to give up our own property, because of love of possessing not because of the necessity of living, and who in addition wish to receive not what might give us the necessities of life but what might increase our possessions by damnable gains?

CHAPTER 15

Covetousness and its domination of those of whom it has once taken possession.

1. Here imperious covetousness orders us, spurning things divine, to concentrate on the ruinous accumulation of earthly possessions so that we place all our solicitude and care in

them, boast of them with unwholesome vanity, neglect to become poor in spirit, being conceited by the greatness of an extensive estate. O crime unheard of! Despising the sweet yoke of Christ, we take on ourselves through a voluntary inclination of our minds the iron rule of covetousness and, disregarding the light yoke of our Lord, which does not oppress its subjects but exalts them, pile on our shoulders a leaden weight which can be dropped more easily than borne; for covetousness, which places this weight on us who freely choose to be enslaved, can be more easily spurned than satisfied and those who have surrendered willingly to their captor will no longer have the will to resist it when it rules them tyrannically. And by a just judgment of God it happens that we who did not wish to resist covetousness when it was on the point of entering can no longer resist it when it has entered.

2. O lamentable servitude of a shamefully conquered mind! O unbearable dominion of fiendish covetousness! In order to bring into its own service as many of its enemies as possible,[44] it promises them amazing things and forces them, wretched and pitiful as they already are, into shameful evils by deceiving them with the promise of earthly goods. It holds us bound by the chains of bittersweet gains and captive as our sovereign; and it does not draw us against our will, but, what is worse, it leads us willing to go wherever it wishes. It ravages in us whatever modesty and sense of shame it finds; and those of us it has already claimed for its triumphs, as though it suspected that we might yet recover our senses, it disarms of all concept of honor: we who were unwilling to resist it must not at any time rebel against it. It carries us off and makes us, greedy for gain, stray through all manners of

acquiring wealth. It does not allow us freedom of mind, nor—with the mind restless and moody—does it permit calm and rest to the body; and like so many cadavers cast out as carrion to birds and beasts of prey, it turns its captives over to unclean spirits to be not merely torn but devoured by the voracious jaws of deadly crimes, yet not so that they cease to live but that they continue to live in torment. In fine, in bodies still alive they carry their own death; that is to say, they are living and dead at the same time. Thence it is that when we live in sin we feel in the pleasure of enjoying carnal things how much an increase in our accumulated wealth delights us; and, being, as it were, dead to virtues, we do not feel what a great poverty of virtues we suffer.

CHAPTER 16

Those possess God more perfectly who renounce earthly possessions from their hearts.

1. This is why it is expedient to hold the goods of the Church, not to satisfy and foster pleasure but to provide for the community life of the brethren and their support so that, while one person shoulders the cares of all living in his company, all those under him may enjoy spiritually a fruitful leisure and quiet. (I inserted that adverb for this reason that if he who enjoys a leisurely quiet does not live spiritually, he lives in the manner of cattle.) And, therefore, he whom no care of bodily need disquiets, no occupation of domestic business distracts, no litigant troubles, no calumniator persecutes: for what else should he be solicitous, being free of these and similar troubles, except that whereby he may become better, lessen his faults by daily improvements, increase his virtues,

and gain possession of spiritual goods in place of the carnal goods he has renounced? Let him exercise himself in these goods with the aid of God, always embrace and love them, and prefer them not only to all his other delights but also to the very torturings [45] of his own flesh, so that he who has left himself nothing that he is afraid to lose may with so great a firmness of faith retain those things for which he has abandoned his possessions that, if necessary, he would willingly give his life for them.

2. Let him, then, whom the pomp of possession entices, with a disengaged heart possess God, who possesses all that He has created, and in Him he will have whatever he holily desires to have. But because no one possesses God save him who is possessed by God, let him first be the possession of God, and God will become his possessor and portion.[46] And who can be more fortunate than he whose Creator becomes his wealth and whose inheritance the very Godhead deigns to be if only he honors Him by holy works, attributes all his success to Him, always lives in and through Him, and possesses nothing earthly along with Him? For the Creator of all, whom nothing of His creation can equal, disdains to be possessed along with the things He has made. In short, what further does he seek whose Maker becomes his all? Or what suffices him whom He does not suffice? That man possessed Him and was possessed by Him, who said in the Spirit: *O Lord, my portion, I have said, I would keep Thy law;* [47] and: *The Lord is the portion of my inheritance and of my cup.*[48] But when He Himself says: *You shall not give to the sons of Levi part among their brethren; I, the Lord, am their portion,*[49] He shows clearly that those who have renounced the portion of an earthly inheritance are entitled to possess God spiritually. Enriched by His gifts, they despise all that

is considered excellent in this world and desire to possess Him and to be possessed by Him, to enjoy Him alone, and to cling inseparably to Him.

3. From this it may be understood that he who pursues and loves temporal goods and worldly joys which will perish, has not learned how numerous are the divine delights. For who can seek anything else whose possession God deigns to be? Or who for His love does not contemn all that is considered great? Let him, then, who wishes to possess God renounce the world so that God may be his blessed possession. But he whom the flattery of earthly possession still attracts does not renounce the world because, as long as he does not renounce his possessions, he serves the world, whose goods he retains; and surely he cannot at the same time serve the world and God. And, therefore, God wished his worshippers to renounce all for which the world is loved, so that, concupiscence of the world having been cast out, divine love could increase and grow perfect in them. And so God ordained that tithes [50] and first fruits, first-born [51] and sin offerings,[52] and gifts which He commanded to be offered to Himself should be distributed to the priests and ministers in order that, while a most devoted people furnished them the necessaries of life, they themselves might minister to their Creator and Shepherd with undisturbed minds and might advance in His worship without any bodily solicitude lest, being enmeshed in earthly occupations, they be unable to take good care of the duties proper to their office.

4. Now, however, that priests of the Christian age manage rather than serve the possessions of the Church, even in this they serve God because, if the things conferred on the Church belong to God, he does the work of God who from the motive

not of any cupidity but of the most faithful stewardship does not neglect the things consecrated to God. Wherefore, the possessions which priests receive from the people should not be considered as to be accounted of the world but of God. For, if the vestments and vessels and other things ministers used for the sacred rites were called holy and could no longer be turned to human use when once consecrated by divine ministers,[53] why should we not consider as holy the things conferred on the Church, which the priests use for necessary purposes, not to serve luxury, as things of the world, but to serve holy ends, as things consecrated to God? Thus, the goods of the Church, collected for this purpose, should serve the needs of all those who place themselves under one person out of love for perfection and do not claim their own for themselves; and whatever progress they make, being freed from all occupation, becomes the fruit of him who alone has been occupied in behalf of many. And, consequently, he who bears responsibility for all who live under him advances in the advancement of his community with the result that, as his occupation has become the fruitful leisure of all his subjects, so their glorious perfection may be considered the honor and glory of their superior.

CHAPTER 17

Those profit nothing who though abstaining from food are slaves of their vices; nor does it avail those who do their own will to renounce their possessions.

1. You also asked what should be regarded as perfection in abstinence, and whether it should be considered necessary only for the body or for the soul as well. If this virtue which

is called abstinence sanctifies the whole man when it is perfect, it is necessary not only for the body but also for the soul because the whole man is composed of body and soul. But in those who, dominated by diverse vices, deny themselves any of the things conceded to our use, this denial should be understood as abstinence, it is true, but carnal and imperfect. On the other hand, that should be regarded as spiritual and perfect which makes the one who abstains hostile to the enticements of carnal pleasures as well as to all sins; one whose soul is not corrupted by the disorders of desires and whose physical strength is not weakened by pleasures sought at the command of an imperious appetite. He, then, is to be considered truly abstinent who has freed himself of all vices, and who, having retrenched his bodily pleasures, strives not to satisfy the concupiscence of his flesh but only to sustain life by taking what is necessary. For, indeed, whatever one takes without which he can live is taken not to sustain life but to foster the luxury of the flesh.

2. This virtue, then, which is called abstinence with regard to abstaining not merely from all dainty foods but also from all evils, although necessary for every single person, is to be considered especially pertinent and proper to those who, according to the practice read of in the Acts of the Apostles, have one heart and one soul,[54] being inflamed by the fire of divine love, and who, living under the rule of one man, have everything in common, provided, however, that they have one life as they have one substance, and that there is no division of minds among those who have their possessions in common. For, in order that a holy union of hearts may be effected and maintained, a fixed sharing of possessions is necessary. Otherwise, what does it avail persons to cast off

their possessions if they do not give up their own will, considering that it is a far more excellent thing to renounce their own will than to renounce their property? Even the philosophers of this world could renounce their possessions,[55] and nowadays some heretics can;[56] but the former, since they were lovers of their own will, did not live according to the will of God, and the latter by insisting on their own will contradict the Lord's will. Consequently, not that which even the enemies of God do commends us to Him but that which is done only by persons who are true Christians and, therefore, lovers of God. These are they who, abandoning their wills and their possessions, subject themselves with all their heart to their Creator and make their will depend on His will and so, being captivated by a love of justice, despise whatever their carnal senses suggest that they should strive for and do.

CHAPTER 18

The first man lost great blessings by his disregard of abstinence.

1. Now, if the first man had willed to keep himself in that happiness of paradise by not eating of the fruit of the one forbidden tree, he would not have lost that state of great felicity, nor would the willful transgression of the saving precept have condemned him to the necessity of corruption and mortality so that he, being corrupted by sin, would either defile or destroy the great benefits of his God which he had received in his original state. For who can adequately recount what great blessings contempt for abstinence took away from him? Being endowed with the dignity of a reasoning mind, he bore the likeness of his Creator; subject to his God alone, he beheld all things subject to himself; by God's

command the fruitfulness of all the trees of paradise served the needs of his life abundantly; [57] the tree of life by the gift of his Creator furnished a mystical food, not to give him life but to prevent his dying; and as long as this food was eaten, it preserved the one who partook of it in one and the same state—thus indicating the figure of a certain sacrament [58]—so that it did not permit him to deteriorate because of any infirmity or to be changed by age and to grow old or to be destroyed by death. Irksome care did not disturb his quiet, anxious labor did not trouble his leisure, sleep did not overtake him against his will, nor did fear of losing his life distress him since he was sure of immortality. He had ready nourishment, a body healthy in every part, emotional tranquillity, a clean heart; he was ignorant of the evil of punishment, a dweller in paradise, unacquainted with sin, fit for God. [59]

2. Lastly, who was happier than he to whom the world was subject, no one hostile, his soul free, and God visible? For, unless before his sin man was accustomed to see God in the assumption of visible creation, how would he, directly he became a sinner, hide from the face of the Lord whom he had never seen? Before his sin, then, Adam could see God just as the Patriarchs saw Him. But when he said: *I heard Thy voice . . . and I was afraid,*[60] he had already fallen from that holy state of seeing God; he had already made himself unworthy to see God. *I heard Thy voice*, he said, *and I was afraid because I was naked; and I hid myself.*[61] Oh, how much security those of good conscience have! And how much the shameful commission of sin humiliates them in their confusion, like those who hid themselves from God's face, confounded by their wickedness, not by their nakedness! They

blushed not because they were exteriorly naked of garments
but because within they were bare of divine protection.[62] In
fact, before their sin they were naked and did not blush [63]
because they had done nothing contrary to the will of God
so that they should feel ill at ease.

CHAPTER 19

*The sin of the first man and the evils which followed his sin
by the judgment of God.*

1. But now, if you will, let us see how those first human
beings committed so great a sin which cast them from paradise into this exile of a life full of grief and in them condemned the whole human race from the beginning. Now,
they would not have eaten of the forbidden tree, so it seems
to me, if they had not been desirous to do so; nor would they
have so desired if they had not been tempted; nor tempted if
they had not been deserted; nor deserted by God if they had
not first deserted Him; [64] nor would they have deserted God
if they had not been proud and had not damnably craved
likeness to God. This they would have acquired without
death of body if, living under God, they had obeyed the
command they had been given, so that they who had in
nature received the possibility of not dying would in glory
attain the impossibility of dying [65] and would there have
obtained the reward of not being able to sin if here it had
been their merit not to want to sin. Hence, open concupiscence would not have moved them, ruined by their striving
after divinity, from their Creator to a creature unless hidden
pride had first seduced them; and the devil would not have
served them such perfidious advice [66] through the serpent if

he had not first ensnared their appetite. *If*, he said, *you shall have tasted of the tree of the knowledge of good and evil, your eyes shall be opened; and you shall be as gods, knowing good and evil.*[67] These are those three things which the Apostle Saint John declares are in the world and must not be loved by the friends of God. He says: *Love not the world nor the things which are in the world; . . . for all that is in the world is the concupiscence of the flesh and the concupiscence of the eyes and the pride of life.*[68] If those who had already fallen away from the love of God had not begun to love these things, never would they have believed the counsel of the serpent, who persuaded them to evil.

2. Thus, concupiscence of the flesh was satisfied by them because they tasted of the forbidden tree; concupiscence of the eyes, because they wished their eyes to be opened; and the pride of life, because they believed they could become the same as God. Seduced, then, by the pleasure of the flesh and the curiosity of the eyes and the pride of life, they were cut off from the tree of life, which gave them the grace of warding off death and of keeping their well-being; and their bodies contracted a diseased condition so that according to the judgment of God they are considered as dead since that day on which in punishment they incurred the necessity of death; and through the tree—which for this reason is called that of the knowledge of good and evil—from which they to their woe failed to abstain when they could, they learned by their penalty what difference there was between the good they had lost and the evil they had incurred; whereas, if, when they had lost so great a good, they had incurred no evil, they perhaps would not have realized what a blessing they had lost. For health becomes more precious when pain tortures; and

the bitterness of illness lends appreciation of health that is lost. And so they began, not by being taught but by experience, to know this evil which it would have been better for them to remain ignorant of, so that from their very misery they might understand how great a happiness they had lost, and that at least the just enduring of the evil of punishment might move those whom the loss of a natural good would perhaps not have moved. These things I have said, by a digression I considered necessary, of the first human beings in order that those who do not wish to undergo the punishment of their damnation may avoid the example of their fall.

CHAPTER 20

Having been restored in Christ, we shall regain all the blessings which we lost when corrupted in Adam.

To be sure, though we were born carnally of Adam, we should nevertheless imitate not him but Christ, in whom we have been reborn and in whom we live when, being renewed to our profit, we lay aside our old way of life. What is it to imitate Adam except to be punished by death for our carnal desires and concupiscences? And what is it to imitate Christ except to be crucified to our carnal concupiscences and desires? In the same way, to lay aside our old way of life is nothing but to live—not according to the flesh, which grows old and dies—but according to God, who alone can continually renew and make happy those who persevere in Him. Wherefore, as when we were in Adam we all fell by his fall, so let us also, since we have begun to be in Christ, who deigned to die for us all, rise spiritually with Him, being dead to sin with Him. In Adam we lost all the blessings we could

7 *

have; in Christ we will receive even greater gifts and gifts that are everlasting if we follow steadfastly in His footsteps.[69] Adam by his guilt rendered us subject to all evils; the coming of Christ freed us from these by His grace. The former transmitted to us his guilt and his punishment; the latter, who, being conceived and born without sin, could not partake in our guilt, by undertaking our punishment effaced both our guilt and its penalty. In a word, Adam took paradise from us; Christ gave us heaven.

CHAPTER 21

The life incumbent on those who desire to imitate Christ.

1. And, therefore, if we wish to be in Him what we should be, as Saint John the Apostle says, *as He walked,*[70] so we also should walk spiritually. What is it to walk as He walked except to contemn all prosperity which He despised; not to fear adversities which He bore; to do gladly what He did; to teach men to do what He commanded; to hope in what He promised; and to follow where He Himself went before? And what is it to follow Him except to show favors even to the ungrateful, not to repay evildoers according to their deserts, to pray for our enemies, to love the good, to compassionate the perverse, to exhort the estranged, to receive in charity those who return, and to tolerate with patience the deceitful and the proud? To this the statement of Saint Paul the Apostle also refers: *If you be risen with Christ, seek the things that are above, where Christ is sitting at the right hand of God.*[71] Those rise with Christ who, like Him, die to sin— with this difference, however, that He died not to His own

sin but to ours. Each of us, on the other hand, dies not to the sin of all but to his own sin.

2. What is it to die to sin except not to live at all to works that condemn one to punishment,[72] to covet nothing carnally, to strive for nothing? Just as one who is dead in the flesh, he who is dead to sin detracts no one any longer; opposes and despises no one; corrupts no one's chastity by clever ruse; shows himself violent to no one; calumniates and oppresses no one; does not envy the good or insult the afflicted; does not serve the luxury of the flesh; does not, being given over to drink, enkindle his thirst more and more by drinking; does not take fire from the torch of hatred; does not pursue unjust gains; does not flatter the powerful or the rich; is not carried away by restless curiosity; is not distracted by the care of domestic business; does not delight in the obsequious salutations of those he meets; is not disturbed by the insults of the haughty. No pride turns his head; windy ambition does not dash him headlong; vainglory does not ignobly torment him; the desire of a brilliant reputation does not inflame him; occupation with another's business does not ensnare him; the love of evil does not entice him to the company of evildoers; the madness of insane anger does not attack him; the desire for sumptuous luxury does not trouble him; the heat of spirited contention does not undo him. No boldness makes him impudent; injustice, unjust; severity, harsh; inconstancy, fickle; contumely, insulting; madness, violent; gluttony, sensual; disobedience, rebellious; boasting, vain; perfidy, unfaithful; levity, light-minded; cruelty, inhuman; shameful appetite, a glutton; restlessness, impatient; instability, unsettled; spiritual infirmity, inconstant; animosity, angry; frowardness, mistrustful; vanity, loquacious; malice, insulting. He

is completely removed from the enticements of earth, removed from uncleanness and enmity, removed from harmful treachery, removed from rapine in the dark and in the open, removed from lying and perjury: removed, in fine, from every manner of shameful excesses and crimes by which those who live carnally offend God and, being dead in sin, do not serve Him. As, I say, one who is dead in the flesh can neither do nor suffer the things I have mentioned, so also the lives of those who, living for God, *crucify their flesh with the vices and concupiscences* [73] have nothing to do with these and similar vices.

CHAPTER 22

The practice of temperance in those who desire to abstain from the pleasure of delicacies or from an immoderate eating of common foods and from an immoderate use of wine.

1. They mortify their *members which are upon the earth* [74] when they chastise their intemperate body by continued fasts, when they keep their appetite within the limit of necessity, when with moderate strictness they not only refrain from the more luxurious foods but even in common foods allow their flesh nothing to satisfy its craving, but only as needed to sustain its life. They are convinced that delicacies are not a detriment if taken without desire, while ordinary foods, if taken with desire, very often harm the progress of abstinence. Hence it is that holy David restrained his craving for water and when his men offered it to him, poured it out in order that it might not appear that he was satisfying his desire for it; [75] on the other hand, the undesired eating of meat did not harm holy Elias. [76] Thus it may be understood that the truly

abstinent condemn not the qualities of foods but concupiscence, and that they mortify their sensuality by not using food or drink which they crave. Those, moreover, who wish to abstain not only in kind but also in amount of food are careful to eat only what seems enough to restore their stomach and to take away hunger. They do not purpose to satisfy their appetite by their eagerness to eat, but restrain it; and not repletion but their will limits their eating. They will repress the desire of the more dainty foods as much as eating common food to excess; they do not wish to enervate themselves by rich foods, the flesh growing unruly, or gorge themselves on common foods; for abstemious men are wont to be neither gourmets nor gluttons.

2. Now, what shall I say of abstaining from wine or of drinking it? In this regard the holy Apostle fixed a sure rule, saying: *Be not drunk with wine, wherein is luxury,*[77] as though he were to say: "An excessive use of wine, not its nature, causes and fosters debauchery; therefore I do not forbid you to use wine, but I forbid you to become intoxicated. For a moderate use of wine strengthens a weak stomach, but drunkenness weakens mind and body." Accordingly, to his disciple Timothy, who had already broken his health by prolonged severe abstinence and had spoiled his stomach by drinking water, he prescribes the use of a little wine, saying: *Do not still drink water, but use a little wine for thy stomach's sake and thy frequent infirmities.*[78] And so people do not violate abstinence who drink wine not with drunkenness in mind but only for the health of their body; whose desire does not proffer it to them but whose infirmity allows it. If such weakness is not present, they should abstain from it; otherwise, the drinking of wine, which strengthens

the sick body, may set aflame a healthy body. For, although no one has called it a sin to use wine or oil, we ought not to give these things to the flesh that desires them for fear that when we begin to yield it things that are permitted, it may demand unlawful things and, since we have humored it in small things, may lead us on to culpable misdeeds; and for fear that the body, confounding the natural order, may not serve the spirit, but the spirit, the body which has the upper hand. Besides, it is a fruit of abstinence that it makes the mind itself alert; it also renders the body agile, not heavy unto lassitude but obedient to the spirit that controls it. The feelings, too, which a surfeit of delicacies is said to make dull and listless, the habit of abstemiousness relieves and refines with the polish, so to speak, of a religious exercise.

CHAPTER 23

The desire of meats, not their nature, defiles those who use meats.

1. If, however, those who abstain from animal flesh enjoy fattened pheasants or other costly birds or fishes,[79] they do not, it seems to me, repress the pleasures of their body but merely change them; and it is not because of abstinence but because of some impurity or, at least—which is closer to the truth—because of the fastidiousness of their squeamish stomachs that they refuse common dainties and ordinary foods. They want the opportunity of satisfying their sensuality not only with different meats but also with those which are more choice and more costly. Here, as I have already shown above, in regard to certain meats which have been given to man to use, we should not condemn their nature, made by God as

they are; but we must flee the carnal concupiscences which the devil has put into the faculties of our flesh. Again, there are those who wish to be regarded as unusually abstemious and eagerly seek glory for themselves because of an ostensibly stricter observance of abstinence; hence, they decide to abstain from all animal foods, only to satisfy the enormous appetite of their body with exotic fruits and exquisite drinks and other such fare; [80] whereas the spirit of abstinence urges not the use of any particular foods but the controlling of desire. Moreover, they should be considered to practice temperance more who deny themselves not the eating of certain things but the enjoyments of the body.

2. Again, those who, while denying themselves the drinking of wine, drown themselves in beakers of various concoctions seem to me not to observe abstinence at all because they keep themselves from wine perhaps so that they may thus purchase the praise of men; and they make up for the wine they deny themselves by the sweeter cups of their pleasures. As regards the use of wine, a person should abstain not from wine alone, but from all that causes drunkenness, or from all that causes, if not drunkenness, at least pleasure, so that he may be perfectly grounded in true abstinence and not imposing in external appearance but hollow within, before men clean, but before God covered with the filth of counterfeit virtue. Nor should we abstain less from the desire to possess superfluities than from the pleasure of eating. For, considering that we have for our use all that we possess, to wish longingly to have those things which one does not intend to use, or even to increase our possessions by gains sought in one way or another, is only to serve, not a necessity to be suffered, but insufferable covetousness. Nor

can I say: "I keep my property so that I may have something to give daily to the poor"; for no one gives more perfectly than he who for the sake of perfection leaves himself nothing of his own.

CHAPTER 24

It is often beneficial to place hospitality to visitors before fasting or abstinence.

1. We should, however, do our abstaining and fasting in such a manner that we do not put ourselves under the necessity of fasting or abstaining; otherwise, we shall be doing an optional thing under constraint rather than out of piety. If, for instance, interrupting my fast, I give refreshment to some visitors, I do not break my fast, but I fulfill a duty of charity. Again, if by my abstinence I sadden my spiritual brethren, who I know derive enjoyment from my unbending myself, my abstinence should be called not a virtue but a vice because continued abstinence and fasting, unless interrupted when occasion requires, actually makes me vainglorious and saddens my brother, whom charity requires me to serve; and it certainly shows that I have no fraternal charity. For charity alone without abstinence makes any Catholic perfect; and abstinence without the addition of charity either brings about the ruin of all or perishes itself.

2. Because, then, even the Manichaeans and some other heretics can practice abstinence and fasting, especially since they detest all flesh not for the sake of abstinence but for uncleanness,[81] and weaken their bodies by living on bread and water, let us not attach any significance to our abstaining from what they also renounce. Let us do so only when

faith commends our abstinence and charity perfects it. Those who do not have these virtues can kill themselves,[82] but they cannot better themselves or become perfect by such abstinence. Let us certainly not think ourselves better because of our abstinence than those Catholic Christians who, whether through being unable to abstain or not wishing to abstain, receive with thanks all that is granted for our use; otherwise, it may be that their humility and other virtues are superior to ours and for that reason they will rightly outrank us who fast. Wherefore, if we wish our abstinence and our fasting to profit us, let us part in the first place with pride, which either drives out or lessens all virtues, and with boasting, the enemy of all virtues; in fact, with all vices whatsoever, so that our abstinence from pleasure-giving foods may benefit us. And then will it benefit us to repress our bodies, or, rather, the evil incitements of our bodies, by the rigor of a strict abstinence if, freed from carnal desires, we flower in holy virtues.

But here let the book conclude. Thus I may in the third volume, with God's help, discuss more extensively and more fully the virtues and the vices on which I have here touched briefly.

BOOK THREE

FOREWORD

In the first volume I dealt with the contemplative life and the questions to what extent the active life differs from it and how you can with the help of God become a sharer in the contemplative virtue itself. In the second book I treated, by God's gift, what I thought should be said of the active life, too: I showed the usefulness of religious rebuke and the virtue of patience and the way the possessions of the Church should be administered and the manner of spiritual abstinence. Now it remains for me to undertake a discussion of the vices and the virtues, not relying on an endowment of which I am not conscious, but assisted by your prayers.

TABLE OF CONTENTS

pulsion keeps from impurity rise to the love of chastity if they accustom themselves to live chastely. 8. The marks by which one can recognize pride, which is either on the surface in the reprobate or concealed in the dissembling. 9. The marks that reveal the envy of the envious. 10. The evils in which vanity involves the vain. 11. The usefulness of fear; it effectually resists sins. 12. The future judgment, the eternity of punishment, and the nature of hell. 13. Praise of charity. 14. An interpretation of what the holy Apostle has said about charity. 15. The perfection conferred by charity on those established in it.

16. The nature of virtue; it permeates those of one mind with it. 17. The rise of the converted to the height of perfection.

18. The perfection to be attributed to the number four; the four virtues called principal, being conferred by God, justify those who live by faith. 19. The nature of temperance and the effect it produces. 20. The type of persons ennobled by fortitude of soul. 21. Justice and, proceeding from it, faith. 22. Equity; the advancement of human society is its concern. 23. The two kinds of injustice. 24. Generosity and the practice of beneficence. 25. The different kinds of love; perfect love as distinguished from them. 26. Giving each man his due. 27. Three virtues—temperance, fortitude, and justice—perfect the active life. Prudence, which is the fourth virtue, furnishes the mind knowledge of hidden things. 28. The social virtue. Those do wrong who do not help human society when they can. 29. From the fount of prudence and wisdom those who are eagerly intent on gaining learning drink knowledge of all things. 30. The prudent neither harm others nor permit themselves to be harmed. They will have

consummate prudence without admixture of any error there where life will be perfect without any sin. 31. The four emotions. These should not be counted among the vices if their use proceeds from a good will. 32. These emotions, without which there is no right living in this life, will not exist in that future happiness, which will have in store neither fear nor sorrow. 33. The four virtues called principal virtues both defend us from sin in the present life and will remain with us forever to the exclusion of every sin. 34. The writer offers an apology for his whole work.

CHAPTER 1

The difference between true virtues and their imitations.

You have asked me to what extent simulated virtues differ from true virtues. I shall not say that the difference is the same as between poison and medicine. Sometimes the curative effect of medicine upon the body is so hampered as to be powerless to defend it from the necessity of death; and as for poison, it does not take life from a body as though it would not have been taken away if poison had not been used, but it only hastens the death of a body which would perhaps have lived a little longer. But I say simply that the difference between imitations of virtues and true virtues is as great as the difference between a lie and the truth. Plainly, the imitation of virtue, which seems to be virtue although it is not, is nothing but a lie and should therefore be called not a virtue but a vice. And real virtue is truth. The person who, having been brought back to life from the death of sin, with devotion applies himself to such virtue can no longer die except when he withdraws from it by reason of a depraved will; just as, on the contrary, the pretense of virtue, which, as I have said, is a lie in opposition to the truth, separates from God, its Life, the soul which will not die but live forever in punishment that is its death, as Scripture says: *The mouth that belieth killeth the soul.*[1] And thus, in the same manner in which virtue, if it is genuine, justifies the soul that truly applies itself to it, so simulated virtue condemns it. And what does justification of the soul mean, if not that its life is everlastingly happy and happily everlasting,[2] just as the soul's condemnation is to be understood as its penalty, and this proves to be death—likewise everlasting?

2. Hence, a soul is doubly guilty if it not only fails to do good, whereby it might live spiritually, but makes a pretense of good, under which it may live badly and hide.[3] The proud man wishes himself to be thought steadfast; the prodigal, liberal; the avaricious, frugal; the rash, brave; the inhuman, humane; the gluttonous, refined; the slothful, retiring; the cowardly, circumspect. Boldness claims the name of confidence, insolence alleges the title of liberty, loquacity imagines itself eloquent, and the evil of inquisitiveness skulks behind the appearance of spiritual zeal. Although it is possible by the aid of human intelligence to recognize these things for what they are, yet without God's gift, so it seems to me, virtues can be neither sought nor possessed, nor can their imitations, made to resemble virtues, be avoided. So true is this that in our opinion infidels derived no advantage even if outwardly they practiced some virtues, because they neither believed that they had received them from their God nor were they willing to refer them to Him who is the end of all good things. Nay—what is this I say: it availed them nothing? The fact is, it even harmed them, as the Apostle says:

All that is not of faith is sin.[4] He did not say: "All that is not of faith has no meaning," but in saying: *All that is not of faith is sin*, he declared that all good things born of faith are virtues, and these surely justify; or, if they are without faith, they should not be considered as virtues but as vices, which do not help those who serve them but condemn them and cast them down in their pride and bar them from the land of eternal salvation.

3. But why do I expatiate on these things that have to do with unbelievers, concerning whom evidently no one is in doubt? Does not the Apostle call carnal even some of the faithful, who, though believing in God, live not according to God but according to men? He says: *And I, brethren, when I came to you, could not speak to you as unto spiritual, but as unto carnal; . . . for you were not able as yet. But neither, indeed, are you now able; for you are yet carnal.*[5] And as though we were going to ask what he intends us to understand by carnal, he promptly adds: *For, whereas there is among you envying and contention, are you not carnal, and walk according to man?*[6] What worse thing can be found than these two scourges of the soul, jealousy and discord, by which even in this life the carnal, who live according to man, are tormented? For discord produces heretics; and jealousy creates imitators of the devil, who envied paradise to the first human beings. And so, when the faithful show delight in justice, piety, compassion, mercy, humility, integrity, and the other virtues, either they live according to God and should be credited with having true virtues, which, when attained, sanctify those who live spiritually and commend them to God; or they live according to man, in which case their virtues are not true virtues but imitations, which do not profit those who live carnally.

4. Therefore, if one who lives religiously, temperately, soberly, and compassionately gives the credit to God, by whose gift he is assisted to live well, he lives according to God—spiritually. If, however, he ascribes to his own strength all that he does well, as though he were sufficient to himself, even without God's help, for doing good, he lives according to man—carnally; and, in consequence, either he does not live well, or whatever good he does for the sake of men does not profit him because, delighted by men's praise, he already receives here the temporal reward of his works, which he did for time. He, therefore, lives according to man who lives according to himself; for he himself evidently is a man [7] and he is living according to himself. If he can do so, he lives with whom he pleases,[8] goes where he pleases, sleeps when and as long as he pleases, eats and drinks when and what and as much as he pleases, laughs and jokes with whom he pleases; in fine, a man who desires carnally all things, lawful and unlawful, cultivates and pursues as he wishes whatever is sweet to his nostrils, soft to his touch, delightful to his eyes, and whatever is pleasing to the other senses of his flesh. But he who lives according to God does not what delights him carnally but what builds him spiritually. He curbs all the cravings of his flesh by delights in spiritual desires. He places future things before present. He subdues the flesh to the spirit; and whatever he desires or does he wishes to proceed not from his own will but from the will of God, whom he longs with all his strength to please.

5. If, then, it has now become fairly clear that they who pretend virtues evidently do not have true virtues, and that they pretend them who do good not from faith or because of God but only because of men, by practicing almsgiving and

fasts or abstinence and the other good works; and who do this not to become good but to pretend to men that they are good; not to receive an eternal reward but to gain popular esteem: let us now see from what prior causes and by what later additions vices usually are engendered and increase, and by what remedies, as by so many medicines, they can with God's help be lessened or corrected.

CHAPTER 2

Pride is the cause of all vices.

1. This is indeed a very involved question; but if you beseech Him who said: *It is not you that speak, but the Spirit of your Father that speaketh in you;* [9] and elsewhere: *Open thy mouth wide, and I will fill it,* [10] the things that are impossible for me as a man become possible when the Lord enlightens and teaches me. Let us, then, consider what causes precede, what vices come after. In order that this might seem more plausible, let not your prudence ask this of me; but by you and by me and by everyone let Divine Scripture be consulted and let it give the reply—the Scripture which, as if we actually were asking it, set forth an unalterable statement, saying: *Pride is the beginning of all sin.* [11] What could be said more clearly, what could be more convincing? *The beginning,* not of some sin, but *of every sin is pride,* it says, in order to show plainly that it precisely is the cause of all sins. Evidently, not only is pride itself a sin, but, furthermore, no sin in the past, present, or future could be committed without it. For all sin is nothing but contempt of God, by which His precepts are trodden underfoot; and that which prompts men to this contempt of God is pride alone.

This it was that caused eternal ruin even in the devil himself, that he should become a devil from being an angel.[12] Then he, knowing that he had fallen from heaven and had been thrust into this prison of the gloomy air [13] because of pride, lured man with a serpent's cunning to the vice of pride in order to subvert him whom God had made without any sin; for the devil was certain that if pride, the cause of all evils, were given entrance, man would then easily commit all sins, conceived as they are only in a proud heart.

2. Hence it is that the first man, seduced by the self-exaltation of a proud spirit, doomed all his posterity, which took its origin from him, to the necessity of corruption and mortality so that, becoming corruptible and mortal, he begot corruptible and mortal beings; and what criminal pride had effected in him thus became the punishment of his sin in all born of him. And, as a result, we cannot now resist sin as could he for whom not to sin was nothing else but not to wish to sin. For us, on the other hand, our desire to live blamelessly is not enough: strength must come to the aid of our will, which fails because of its feebleness. In his case a nature still sound could even help him not to sin, whereas ours, being now vitiated, hinders us; and the will to sin alone made him sin, but the necessity that has now been made of sin very often forces us. Wherefore, we cry to God and say: *Deliver me from my necessities.*[14] And when Divine Scripture says: *Pride is the beginning of all sin*, it is perhaps for this reason that it came first in the devil and through him man was perverted, concerning whom the Apostle says: *By one man sin entered into the world, and by sin death; and so death passed upon all men, in whom all have sinned.*[15]

3. But we who sinned in the sin of the first man, not in

8 ⁴

our present individual life but in his nature in which we existed, contracted corruption from his disease of corrupt pride as if from a root; and in this our corruption we have all the causes of sins. We do not become corrupt because we sin; but because we are corrupt, we commit every sin from this corruption of ours. The first man, however, did not sin because he was corrupt; but when he was incorrupt, he corrupted himself by sinning and transmitted his corruption to us.[16] And hence, there where we shall be without any sin, all our mortality and our entire corruption which resulted from sin must needs be removed; while here, where our nature, weakened by sin, has not as yet been restored but is still being healed by grace, our pious efforts are opposed by that base concupiscence which is not according to nature, but which has been imposed and engrafted on our nature as a punishment—a concupiscence which was caused by sin and which causes sin if it conquers. Although we have this concupiscence as long as we live as mortals, nevertheless, let us not support it with the desire of our will, and we shall conquer; for not by feeling it in us but by consenting to it do we sin; nor does it conquer us the moment it assails us, but only if—may that not happen!—it casts our mind down from the sublimity of its resolve into consent to sin.

CHAPTER 3

Pride, from which all vices proceed, is overcome by the virtue of humility; and all vices are routed and perish as they yield to virtues.

1. If, then, pride is the beginning of every sin and concupiscence is the punishment of sin, evil concupiscence can-

not be overcome unless pride is first guarded against by the virtue of humility, which is its enemy. A proud will causes the commands of God to be despised; a humble will causes them to be obeyed. Pride made demons of the angels; humility renders men like to the holy angels. The former makes rebels who are subject to the devil; the latter joins the humble to Christ. The proud desire that what they do not perform be praised in them; the humble shun recognition of their good deeds. The former excuse the perversity of their wills by disclaiming their vices; and by crediting their virtues to their own strength they boast shamefully. The latter, if they commit any sin, accuse themselves by confessing it voluntarily; and by attributing all the good that is in them to God's divine bounty they continually praise Him. Therefore, if virtue does not abide in a wicked mind, let pride yield to the sway of humility because the soul cannot harbor the reign of virtues unless it has first struck off the yoke of vices. But then only do vices depart if they are firmly cast out and made to give place to virtues. Otherwise, if virtues have not taken the places of the vices which have been expelled, these bide their time and return.

2. Therefore, let gentleness oppose cruelty in us; let resolute patience check anger; chastity overcome lust; calmness take away wrath; discreet silence repress loquacity; spiritual delight lessen carnal desires; the rigor of abstinence blunt the stings of the flesh;[17] spiritual eagerness replace curiosity; drunkenness yield to sobriety; clemency master cruelty; seriousness[18] overcome levity. As the love of God and neighbor increases, let all concupiscence of the world be destroyed; let true moderation keep out luxury; the virtue of industry correct sloth; deep humility bridle pride; unsophisticated sim-

plicity drive out folly; let fickleness be routed and not hamper constancy; let faultless morals strengthen discipline, considerate mercy soften harshness, and acquired goodness utterly root out evil: so that by the expulsion of vices the glorious entrance of virtues may be proclaimed. But we shall consider the virtues in a chapter to follow; now let us continue with the vices as we have begun.

CHAPTER 4

Cupidity. This is so mixed with pride that no sin is committed which does not proceed from both.

1. If it has now become sufficiently clear how the Scriptural saying should be understood: *Pride is the beginning of all sin,*[19] let us also examine this statement of the holy Apostle: *The desire of money is the root of all evils.*[20] Since the Holy Spirit, who spoke through the Prophet, spoke also through the Apostle and cannot contradict Himself, we should carefully consider why the one chose to call pride the beginning of all sin and the other, the desire of money the root of all evil. Or was the Apostle Paul perhaps commenting, as was his custom, on the words of the Prophet? For, whether you say *the beginning of all sin* or *the root of all evils,* you mean one and the same thing. Covetousness and pride are indeed a single evil inasmuch as no proud man can be found without covetousness, and no covetous person without pride. Thus, even the devil, in whom pride holds the mastery, was covetous of his own power and of man's ruin; [21] and man himself, by his desire of the forbidden tree and his striving after the likeness of God, showed the passion of diseased covetousness. For out of pride are born heresies,[22]

schisms, detractions, envy, talkativeness, boasting, strife, enmity, ambition, haughtiness, presumption, vanity, irritability, lying, perjury, and other such vices. But who doubts that these come from covetousness, too, since everyone who has been corrupted by any one of the diseases I have named is regarded as covetous also?

2. Likewise, since covetousness makes gluttons, libertines, drunkards, misers, thieves, fornicators, adulterers, perverts, incestuous men, profligates: how can they be made such without pride, without which they cannot at all contemn the precepts of God which forbid all those evils I have enumerated above? Therefore, if we wish to complete victoriously the course of our struggle,[23] let us beware in the first place of covetousness and pride—not two vices but one—from which all evil acts have their origin. For without pride what sin can even begin to exist since it is said: *Pride is the beginning of all sin?* Or without covetousness, which is *the root of all evils*, what evils can be committed since without root all things are counted as naught or dead? If, then, I cannot commit any sin unless I consent to the evil pleasure, which is the essence of covetousness, and contemn God's precepts, which is the evil of pride, is it not evident that every sin proceeds from covetousness, *the root of all evils*, and from pride, which is called *the beginning of all sin?*

CHAPTER 5

The torment of mind with which envy afflicts the envious.

Of course, the envious one who by envy makes the good of another his own punishment, seems not to be tempted to envy by any covetousness but only to be troubled by the disease of pride.[24] But if you examine carefully and thoroughly the plague by which his soul is inflamed and brought low, you will find that he is held both by a desire for the damnation of the man whose death he wishes and by the evil of pride, whereby he continually grieves that the better man, whom he envies, is preferred to him. Who can easily express in words what an evil this is whereby the envious through hatred of a man attacks the divine good in him, when he should rather be loved, and that, too, in proportion to the holiness of his merit? The envious man has by just punishment as many tormentors as the envied man had praisers. Indeed, excellence of merit makes a man envied; the punishment of sin makes him envious. Nor can man apply a remedy to him whose wound is hidden.

CHAPTER 6

The vices into which concupiscence of the flesh breaks out when a corrupt mind consents to it.

1. As to the man given over to concupiscence of the flesh, does he perhaps appear to have no pride, considering especially that the very suffering of his lust seems to humble him? However, if he had not first rebelled against God, whose saving precept on preserving chastity he contemns by the presumption of a proud spirit, no wanton desire would tempt him to impurity. In his soul there takes place a long struggle between contempt and fear of God, and either contempt of God gets the upper hand, and his proud soul, letting in carnal desire, loses its chastity; or fear prevails, and his soul, being

subject to God, rebuffs carnal desire and pride at the same time.

Now, gluttony and an abundance of wine shamefully lull many into impurity; evil thoughts inflame others to the harm of their purity; occasions they meet cast some from their resolution of chastity; and some others the example of libertines places under the yoke of impurity.

2. There are others whose soul a base tongue sears [25] or whose base conscience it reveals, who first either take pleasure in using impure language or in listening to it and then, as the disease gradually spreads, abandon their honor. With their sense of shame destroyed, they become vile, and, though in their indecency they wish to be regarded as elegant, they now without regard for anything shamelessly mouth their foul talk. For every man speaks of what he holds dear, and he hears with pleasure what he dwells on in his thoughts. Now, thought it is which, if it is decent, chastens the mind, the same as evil thought defiles it; or rather, if the condition of the mind does not come from thought but the quality of thought from the mind, sordid thought does not make a mind sordid, but from a sordid mind arise sordid thoughts. If this is so, the forms of beautiful bodies, stealing in through the eyes, do not trouble an incorrupt soul; and when they do excite a soul corruptibly, they do not corrupt a healthy soul but reveal one corrupt by its own choice.

3. Vile words, too, which enter through the ears, what peculiar strength have they if they have not been freely admitted by the mind? But when they do prevail, they do not corrupt that mind but find it already corrupt of its own free will. For to chaste ears obscene talk vanishes with the sound and does not invade the sanctuary of a pure heart. The soft

caress which tempts a mind already vitiated [26]—can this receive admission to the soul through touch if the soul keeps inviolate the resolve of its professed faith? [27] Actually, then, the soul, vitiated by its own will, first loses its integrity and so admits the pleasure of the touch. Of avoiding the pleasure of food and drink I have already said enough, I think, in the second volume, in which I recommended with all possible brevity the perfection of spiritual abstinence.

4. But here, too, I say this briefly: the delight of the palate does not break into the mind through the mouth of flesh, nor does shameful speech break forth from the mind unless the mind corrupts itself voluntarily before it receives or brings forth anything that might corrupt it. But if the soul continues firm under its God by the same God's gift and does not yield to any seductive pleasures, it neither brings forth nor receives anything evil.

And now I shall make a few remarks about odors, in order that I may include in my discussion every temptation of the five senses. These odors, coming through the nostrils, the weak mind either desires or by divine aid spurns. If it subjects itself to its Creator and lovingly clings to Him who is its dignity and salvation, not only does no stain of vices tarnish it, but no carnal pleasure unmans it. If, however, the soul wantonly withdraws from the love of its Creator and Enlightener [28] and, renouncing a good of intrinsic worth, throws itself upon extrinsic goods, whatever stamina it possesses is dissipated and all its strength is weakened and broken. And then spiritual activity becomes burdensome to it and it becomes restlessly occupied with carnal things so that it basely desires all it feels through bodily sensation, not on the point of being corrupted but already corrupt; and when the body feels no sensible objects, the soul represents to itself by pleasure-giving recollection the images of sensible things. Within itself it hears, without voice, whatever beguiling song and obscene joke have flowed through the tortuous windings of the ears. There the evilly sweet odor which has crept in through the receptive hollows of the nostrils is seductively fragrant to it. There the sàvor admitted through the enticement of a voluptuous palate delights it. There it feels vividly any softly alluring sensation that external touch has impressed upon it. There it sees with longing various colors and seductive figures which the curiosity of its eyes has reported to it.

5. Such a mind, made carnal, very often so delights in the phantasms of bodies when bodies are absent that, fascinated through the extreme vividness of its evil thought, it seems to itself to embrace not imaginary but real bodies. And so, that flux of the body which occurs in sleep without guilt sometimes happens culpably to those awake. For what occurs in sleep is one thing; what one does when awake is another. In the former state the fullness of humor is expelled naturally; in the latter, it is evilly brought forth by concupiscence. But this concupiscence in waking hours calls forth this flux in persons whose base appetite it has aroused through obscene talk. They are the ones who go into details about women: this one is awkward, that one, coquettish; this one is homely, that one, beautiful. The finery of one, the carriage of another, give pleasure. Gaiety, even without beauty, is praised in one; beauty alone, in another. Thence they pass to morals: to such people moderation in speech commends one woman; boisterous freedom makes another seem wicked. In making these and similar things the topic of their conversation these

men furnish material for their own concupiscence. They are not lustful, however, for the mere reason that they like to speak of, or listen to, these things: unless they were already corrupted by the passion of concupiscence, they would never say such things or listen to them; for these things do not corrupt them but show them as corrupt.

6. And lest anyone think that I should be criticized for candidly reproving such conduct, let him know that it was perhaps for this reason that the ancients decreed that no youths should read the Book of Genesis and also part of the Prophet Ezechiel and the Canticle of Canticles [29] and other such writings, in which the generations and deeds and names of certain women have been recorded. Though we believe these women had historical existence, we understand, nevertheless, that their names symbolize virtues because, just as they not only delighted their husbands by their good morals but also, without loss of modesty, charmed those not of their household by their very great beauty, so holy virtues render their possessors admirable to all their own and strike those who do not possess them with a certain admiration. That is why even those who live badly give precedence to virtues before vices; for what they do because of their passions is one thing, what they are forced to approve by their judgment is another. But lest perhaps those who were still carnal should receive these spiritual things according to the flesh and not think upon the virtues which these women represent but become enamored of them by thinking carnally of the women themselves, rightly were the young forbidden to read those passages. Though they give life when they are spiritually received, yet when the mentality itself is carnal, it uses them to furnish the carnal-minded occasions for carnal concupis-

cence. Such a person frequently has their names on his lips; he bears in his smitten heart a desire for them and in his soul holds pent up all the evil he is ashamed to put into practice, guilty in the judgment not of men but of God.

CHAPTER 7

Even those whom some compulsion keeps from impurity rise
to the love of chastity if they accustom themselves
to live chastely.

Restraint placed upon the body makes such persons chaste, or the fear of temporal punishment keeps them from an act of impurity, or opportunity is denied them. But although he who is chaste by compulsion is impure in will, yet if the man of temperate body thanks God, the Author of all natures, for the gift of his nature; and if the man whom fear keeps in the possession of chastity and the man who is denied the opportunity for adultery grow accustomed to live chastely: they very often advance to virtue through necessity; and, little by little, as the charm of purity increases, they become truly chaste and advance so far that, showing hatred for the baseness of impurity not by word of mouth but by virtue, they no longer resist carnal seductions from fear of punishment, which is characteristic of beginners; but from detestation of sin they bridle the unruly passions of the flesh, and this is the height of consummate chastity. Not that the soul could ever in this life cease to combat vices; but the very frequency of its victories supports it and leads it on and, to the extent this is possible in the present life, perfects it. Only, it must not let itself be captivated by the delight of sensible things and cast itself down to the level of the body; but, sublimely strengthened by the renunciation of pleasures, in victory over material things it should rise above the body and cling to its God, under whose protection the desires that are spurned cannot vanquish it during life—to be glorified forever.

CHAPTER 8

The marks by which one can recognize pride, which is either on the surface in the reprobate or concealed in the dissembling.

1. Now, then, let us see by what marks pride can be detected. Thus, as in the preceding it became clear that without it no sin can be committed, here I purpose to show the signs whereby it can be recognized and avoided. I say nothing about those whom their very appearance and walk reveal as proud. Their unbending neck, harsh expression, piercing eyes,[30] and frightening manner of speech shout undisguised pride. Possessed by the lust of dominating, they use violence to subject those whom they can, confound human and divine right, are bloated by honors, appropriate everything everywhere, rejoice in their crimes, and, corrupted by the passion of pride, find themselves too small for themselves. These, then, I pass over—people in whom pride rules so openly that it neither deigns to hide nor can it. Those wretches alone I speak of, and I warn against their examples as examples to be avoided, who, when already converted and making a little progress, are secretly ensnared by pride, cast into an abyss of woes by its deceitful domination and continually trampled underfoot to keep them from ever again raising themselves up. In the hearts of such men pride makes

room for the devil; as he comes, it throws open to him, as to one with family rights, the unguarded heart; receives him as he enters; proclaims the law of evil living to the prisoners it holds; takes away the armor of virtues from all whom it has overpowered; stifles whatever remains in them which could offer resistance to vices, to prevent them from recovering strength against it.

2. Thence it is that those whom the festering disease of a proud mind has corrupted do not obey the orders of their superiors but sit in judgment on them. Rebuked for their negligence, they either rebel insolently or murmur. They contend for the higher place; wish impudently to be preferred even to their betters; mockingly criticize the simplicity of their spiritual brethren; air their views shamelessly; are bored by the attention shown them; seek obstinately the attentions denied them; prefer high birth to morals; highhandedly despise their juniors; do not believe that any person can be compared to them; disdain to be made equal with their elders; place themselves above them solely on the strength of their soul's conceit. They do not observe reverence in obedience, modesty in speech, discipline in manners. They remain stubborn of purpose, hard-hearted, boasting in their conversation. They are deceitful in their humility, obstinate in hate, impatient of subjection, covetous of power, hateful to all the good. They are slothful in doing a good work,[31] disagreeable in company, difficult to oblige. They are quick to speak of what they do not know, prompt to trip up others, unfeeling in regard to all things on which brotherhood subsists; rash in daring, vociferous in speech, bored by listening, presumptuous in teaching, crudely immoderate in laughter, a nuisance to friends, a threat to the peaceful, ungrateful for favors, inflated by attentions, and overbearing towards subjects.

3. These are the marks of raging pride, which offend God and cause Him to depart and to abandon proud hearts. Feeding on these evils, the devil exults. He is invited to come; he enters proud minds to master them; raises them up to dash them down; pampers them to destroy them. Because of this captivity of the wicked he dances with insatiate glee: that he should be the lawful master of prisoners whom he has subjected by the weapon of pride and through whom he can work all the evils I have enumerated above! Rightly, then, by the just judgment of God are they abandoned, condemned as they are to such a punishment of which they are not aware, because they have not been made bondsmen by force, but of their own will they surrender to the rule of deceitful pride; and this they surely can resist, if they wish, by the choice of their free will since they have been freed and fortified by the gift of the Holy Spirit. But even such men, if they conceive the hope of regaining salvation, being inspired by God to recover it, and do not in despair abandon themselves in their sins, can be healed by the medicine of salutary repentance and can by acquiring deep humility be released from the chains of eternal damnation, if they condemn the pride which has thrust them, swollen with it, from their God. How this can be done I have already said in treating of pride itself: whence it proceeded, whither it came, and what it did. For it proceeded from the devil, came to the first man, and in him corrupted the whole human race, as the fruit in the root, by the corruption of a nature that sinned of its own free will.[32]

CHAPTER 9

The marks that reveal the envy of the envious.

Right order requires me, I think, to say a few words also about envy, which has flowed from the fount of pride in so far as the devil, who perished by pride, burning with the poison of envy, promptly caused the ruin of the first man; yes, indeed, it was from the devil that envy proceeded. Accordingly, since this same devil showed himself envious through pride—not proud through envy—pride was not the fruit of envy, but envy proceeded from the root of pride. That is why, since my previous discussion has already shown how much envy afflicts the envious, I think I should not in this place speak of the punishment of envy, whereby the envious harrow and kill their own souls. But, the Lord granting, this alone I ought to show: how the envious through envy make the merits of those who live holy lives their own sins; and how greatly envy corrupts the good in those who either discredit entirely whatever good they hear holy persons have done or said, or turn good deeds into evil by interpreting them unfavorably. Every evil which lying rumor has intimated about the good they immediately believe as though they themselves had seen it. Maliciously they contradict those who would prove to them that it is not true. They imagine everything of their rivals, fret over their advancement. They harbor secret hatreds, and even against those of their own family they foment trouble. They envy those who do good, but think highly of those who sin. They rejoice in the misfortunes of the good, grieve over their successes, burn with unprovoked enmities, fearing the while that the evil of their heart will be discovered. They are always bitter, never knowing what they want. They are friends of the devil, enemies even of themselves, hateful to all. They are troubled in joy, joyful in sorrow—perverse in both respects. Among friends they sow discord; they confirm in dissension, if they can, those who are temporarily at disagreement. They defame the reputation of the good by means of lies. In spiritual men they praise carnal things, having in mind to persuade them that they lack spiritual goodness. They pretend friendships to trick with what cunning they can those who have incautiously entrusted themselves to them. They increase their occasions of hatred by evil suspicions. They give joy to the demons, whose works they pursue; they sadden holy men who know them. By courtesy they would be friends, but in their souls they are enemies.[33] They are chaste of speech, but base in their actions. They are prodigal of secrets, tenacious of wrongs, prompt to evil suspicions. Empty of goodness, they are full of meanness, gifted for deceit. At heart they are enemies of virtues, depraved in morals, and treacherous to all who live with them in uprightness.

2. These and similar characteristics show that all the envious are enemies, heart and soul, of the good. Into these evils do those fall who, by censuring those they should follow and by hating those they should love, spitefully shut themselves off from the society of all upright persons so that the good they persecute in the good is justly not in them. Consider, I beg you, how their own evils will afflict the envious, who are afflicted even by the goods of others. Where will those who are evil in good be able to become good? Or when will they use evils well who do not cease to use good things badly? The holy martyrs used evils well,[34] steadfast in wit-

ness to our Savior and doughty fighters in spiritual warfare. Afflicted and at the same time proved by tribulations and loss and by a variety of tortures, they exchanged earthly goods for heavenly; and, beginning with a good use of evils,[35] they arrived at the joys of everlasting blessings. Similarly, the envious man uses good things badly because, separated from all the good which in his wretchedness he abhors, he will be left to be punished by the torture of his soul. And who will be able to help the man who through envy sets himself up as his own tormentor? Or whence will he contrive salvation for himself who, by using good things badly, draws damnation from the material of salvation? Yet if the envious, too, like other sinners, rise by divine inspiration to the hope of regaining salvation and are displeased with themselves as they are because they wish to please God; if they do not imitate Cain, who, having wickedly killed his brother in blindness caused by the frenzy of overpowering envy, and having consigned his soul, branded with fratricide, to the punishment of everlasting death, being oppressed by despair of gaining pardon, said to the Lord: *My iniquity is greater than that I may deserve pardon* [36]—which is to say to God: " I do not ask You to forgive me because the greatness of my sins surpasses the greatness of Your pardon," and, accordingly, never does one read that he either repented his crime or merited pardon: if, then, the envious, shunning such an example, withdraw from themselves and restore themselves to God and do not leap into the abyss of woes through despair of their salvation, who doubts, nay, who does not firmly believe, that they can receive pardon for their former wickedness if only, being cured and healed of the wound of envy,[37] they drive bitterness from their souls by the sweetness of brotherly love, sincerely loving those whom they formerly

9 ‘

hated so that they may be helped to the good of fraternal union and peace by the example of all the good whose merits were formerly a source of annoyance to them?

CHAPTER 10

The evils in which vanity involves the vain.

1. Now that I have made these remarks about envy, I shall show in the following section in how serious an evil vanity, too, entangles the vain. In order that vanity may be more readily avoided, let me show briefly what depravity it contains in itself. Now, vanity is a certain conceited passion of a listless soul for manifold pleasures. Vanity is greedy to gain honors and at the same time ignorant as to how to acquire them. It is flushed by the fever of pretended superiority—hollow, morbid, moody. It dominates the light-minded, charms all the shiftless; it fumes at those who show disagreement, courts those it would captivate, and is invincible once they have yielded to capture. It is a type of simulated virtue, the soul of vices, tinder for carnal pleasures, the ruin of morality, the passion for honors. It dotes upon the wicked, is galled by the perfect, brings the irresolute into danger, is imperious to its subjects, and has only weakness to offer to the strong. It finds it easy to make captives, fascinates those it has captured, pricks the ambitious, turns the head of the narrow-minded, brings humiliation upon the haughty. The proud are its slaves; at its feet lie the self-exalting; the desperate try to find it; those who face ruin run to it; and, ruined, they fancy that in its possession they stand in security.

2. This is vanity, which, as we consider it, not merely

saps certain virtues, but when it has been given entrance by the wicked, consolidates the despotism of vices. But it finds no entrance in minds that are filled with virtues. Empty persons, then, and those supported by no virtue it tempts; and by a certain delight in raging in the open, it plunges those who are puffed up by the arrogance of ruinous ambition into secret vices, just as a storm tosses an empty vessel to and fro on swollen waves and as on a threshing floor the wind carries off the light chaff while the grain remains of its own weight. If this is so, vanity does not corrupt men but reveals their corruption. It tosses them around by the wind of its breath and spins and whirls them around by shifting desires. By the bent of their own will they conform themselves to all its caprices. They boast shamefully of works of which they are not conscious; wrongly pretend to enjoy the approbation of all; depreciate holy men in comparison with themselves. Carrying their heads high because of popular favor, they judge themselves as lacking no perfection. They delight in the obeisances of those they meet, bestow favor on those who flatter them, follow their passions, make themselves acceptable to all the wicked. They have a penchant for teaching what they do not know, wish sublime things to be believed of them, and place pleasure before serious matters. They abominate in speech what they desire in their hearts. To their vices they give the names of virtues. They deceive themselves, deceive those who befriend them. They are quick to make noble promises, but show themselves liars in keeping them. Unstable in good, they are tenacious of evil. Serious in speech, they are base of soul—always deceivers. They are full of joy in prosperity, without strength in adversity. Made arrogant by compliments, they are depressed under reproaches. Knowing no moderation in joys, they are eager for the things of the world, but always reluctant in virtuous matters.

3. Vanity, therefore, pursues those who are marked by these and similar faults and does not allow them either to notice their disease or to have recourse to a physician. And what else is it to go to a physician than that the sick person recognizes his illness and is not pleased with himself but is shaken by acts that used to seem glorious to him? Those persons, certainly, do not act thus who, inflamed with the desire of winning a reputation, apply themselves only to those works which buy human approval and who contemn moral goods. And so much does their eagerness for human praise obsess them that unconcernedly they undertake and readily carry out laborious, wearisome projects for the people to admire and to spread their reputation. Hence it is, too, that fasting, abstinence, nightly vigils, churchgoing, and the chanting of psalms, although all these things are done not without effort, are undertaken even with pleasure by such as wish to please men thereby. This of course does not imply that men of God do not also do these things; but that those who desire fervently to excel also in holy morals are known to present them to God rather than to men.

4. But if a man is resplendent without, where he can be considered great, and is filthy within, where God alone sees, who does not understand that all his continued labors of abstinence, fasts, and watchings, which love of God makes bearable for us but love of human praise and burning vanity make tolerable for him, are not the ornaments of his virtues but the cloak of his vices? Wherefore, true fasts, vigils, almsgiving, and other good works of this kind ought to increase our virtue, not serve to hide our sins; and they should be

shown to God not in place of right living but along with right living; for those who through love of perfection are prepared to go beyond the precepts should certainly carry them out with far greater care. On the other hand, if the envious, the proud, the arrogant, the covetous do not repress these and similar evils of their heart and yet wear out their body by fasts and by the labors of abstinence however prolonged, the works done for vanity do not justify them, and the vices of which they fail to rid themselves condemn them.

And now, in this book I have, it is true, regularly added after the treatment of each vice also the remedies by which it can be prevented or cured. Still, here I should, the Lord enlightening me, summarize and set up some rule whereby those who make a genuine effort to be guided by it may resist all sins: nothing so keeps us immune from every sin as the fear of punishment and the love of God. But in regard to charity I shall discuss this later as the Lord will grant me, whose gift this charity is.

CHAPTER 11

The usefulness of fear: it effectually resists sins.

Now let me say a few things about the fear of punishment. Let a soul before it sins look to the penalty that is due to sin. Let it weigh against carnal enticements the torture and anguish that usually pursue the sinner, and no sin will please it nor will any carnal delight tempt it to sin. In fact, we yield to our temptations and passions not because we cannot resist them but because we promise ourselves security in hiding our sin; and since we believe that we can gloss over or buy off our deeds, being tempted by the hope of a pre-

sumed impunity, we permit our passion to dominate over us.
But if, at the time he is deliberating about a sin, a man were
to consider with a calm mind what penalty awaits those who
are caught in their sins and wickedness, what punishments
torture them when convicted, what trembling palsies their
limbs,[38] what pallor suffuses their countenance,[39] and, finally,
how much the shame of an evil repute humiliates them and
makes them hateful to all, I do not know whether he could
consent to any sins whatsoever. For what evil deed can be
committed which does not cause a blush even to those whom
their own sins delight? Thence it is that those who vainly
and disgustingly vaunt their good deeds hide the sins which
trouble and humiliate them. Is it not true that even without
human judgment the torments of an accusing conscience rage
against a sinner and even the thoughts of secret guilt afflict
with painful remembrance a soul that realizes its baseness?

CHAPTER 12

*The future judgment, the eternity of punishment, and the
nature of hell.*

1. Now consider this: when we shall come to the Last
Judgment to be sentenced by that Judge whom we can
neither deceive by the concealment of crimes [40] nor corrupt by
the offer of any gift to promise impunity; [41] when the secrets
of all begin to be revealed,[42] and not only our deeds and words
but even our very thoughts begin to be shown: what shall we
do before the majesty of so great a Judge? What excuse
shall we be able to offer? With what kind of defense shall
we clear ourselves? What penance, which we contemned
in this life, will help us? What good works, which we did

not perform in this life, will defend us? To what Apostles or to what other holy saints, whose examples and words we despised, shall we flee?

But perhaps frailty of body will there excuse some. Their defense, however, will be repudiated by the examples of all the saints. Living in the flesh with the frailty of the flesh, conquering the frailty of the flesh in the flesh, the saints have taught that what they did surely can be done; and this especially because they resisted sin not through their own virtue but through the help of the merciful Lord, who shows Himself to those who do not seek Him [43] so that they may seek Him and believe in Him and who defends with His invincible protection those who believe in Him that they may not be overcome by sin.

2. What, then, will sinners reply if the Lord says to them: "If you were able, why did you not resist the desires of sins? If you were unable, why did you not seek my aid against sins? Or if you were wounded, why did you not by repentance apply a remedy to your wound?" Will He not, when they are silent at this and have no excuse to offer, say: *Bind them hands and feet and cast them into exterior darkness; there shall be weeping and gnashing of teeth;* [44] *where their worm shall not die and their fire shall not be quenched?* [45] And what does it mean for them, as they stand silent, to be bound hands and feet if not to be deprived of doing good [46] in hell, where no one confesses God? So, too, to be sent into exterior darkness will be nothing else but to be banished from the Lord, who is the Light of minds. [47] The weeping and the gnashing of teeth, moreover, represent the most poignant anguish of those who, delivered over to the punishment of eternal death, are destined to experience not sight [48] but pain.

Their continued lamentation, eternal torment, extreme anguish, and consciousness of punishment rack their souls but do not destroy them, punish their damned bodies but do not annihilate them. The unquenchable fire does not kill those consigned to it for this reason, that, with the life of sensation remaining, their punishment may remain and keep them who are fettered to eternal bodies and whom an undying second death [49] slays with live flames, in a state of pain rather than of life. Further, *their worm shall not die and their fire shall not be quenched* refers to the whole punishment of the damned, whom the fire of useless repentance burns and the worm of a consuming conscience everlastingly gnaws. Accordingly, when it is said regarding all those who are in hell that they are "slain," this does not imply that they may at some time cease to exist, having been consumed by their extreme pains, but that it is their penalty to live in pain.

3. To be willing to hear or read these and similar things; continually to bring them before the eyes of the mind; to believe that they will happen; to fear without any anxiety; to consider what an evil it is to be excluded from that joy of the divine contemplation; to be deprived of the blessed society of all the saints; to become an exile from the heavenly homeland; [50] to die to a happy life; to live an everlasting death; to be thrust into eternal fire with the devil and his angels where a second death is the exile of the damned and their life is pain; in that fire not to see that which gives light; to experience that which causes torture; to suffer the terrible crackling of the welling flames; to be blinded by the biting fumes of the reeking abyss; to be immersed in the depths of the seething inferno; to be forever gnawed by voracious worms and not to die; to meditate on these and many like

things is only to renounce all vices and to bridle all carnal pleasures.

But now, if you will, let us rise from these terrible evils which strike the minds of the faithful with a healthy terror and which draw them away from all vicious pleasures—evils which those who love their passions will then make trial of by their own damnation when, more pitiable than any misfortune, they can no longer change their lives—from these terrifying and lamentable evils let us rise, I say, to those lofty things by which the minds of those who make progress ascend to the hope of attaining happiness and, abjuring earthly things, long for those of heaven. And because they who desire to advance begin with salutary fear and, by making progress, arrive at charity, let me, now that I have, I think, said enough about the fear of beginners, also treat charity as He whose gift it is, will grant me.

CHAPTER 13

Praise of charity.

Charity is, so it seems to me, a right will turned completely from all earthly and present things, joined and united inseparably to God, inflamed by a certain fire of the Holy Spirit, from whom it comes and to whom it is referred. Charity is foreign to every defilement, impervious to corruption, subject to no defect of changeableness, exalted above all that is carnally loved, powerful over all the emotions, eager for divine contemplation, always unconquered in everything; it is the perfection of good deeds, the boon of morality, the end of heaven's precepts, the death of crimes, the life of virtues, the strength of warriors, the palm of victors, the soul of holy minds, the source of good merits, the reward of the perfect. It brings back to life those who are dead in their sins, heals the sick, restores the lost, inspires hope in the desperate, abides in peaceful minds. It is fruitful in those repenting, joyful in those making progress, glorious in those persevering, victorious in the martyrs, full of works in every one of the faithful. Faith conceives it, hope flies to it, the increase of all the virtues serves it; and from it every good work draws its life. Under it obedience grows, through it patience conquers, because of it religious devotion spurns carnal enticements. Without it no one has pleased God; with it no one has been able to sin nor will he be able. This is true charity, genuine, perfect charity, which the holy Apostle calls *a more excellent way.*[51] And, truly, it is the way which leads those who walk by it to their homeland because, just as no one arrives at his destination without a road, so without charity, which is called a way, men cannot walk but only go astray.

CHAPTER 14

An interpretation of what the holy Apostle has said about charity.

1. Now, then, let us learn what this charity is and how great it is—the way not of our feet but of our morals, as the Apostle teaches. *If,* he says, *I speak with the tongues of men and of angels, and have not charity, I am become as sounding brass or a tinkling cymbal.*[52] By tongues of men and of angels we ought to understand him to mean the empty oratory of certain men who speak whatever they wish, correctly, it may be, and eloquently; but, however excellent the style and

the content of their speech, nevertheless, if they undertake the office of teaching from vanity of pleasing more than from love of counseling; not to teach others, but to show that they are learned; not to seek the advancement of their audience but to strive for their applause; if with evil wit they transfer all their conscience's concern to their tongue and aspire more earnestly to improve their eloquence than their way of life; if in the conceit of their empty loquacity they desire their words to be praised rather than to be acted upon; if they are solicitous not for the holiness of their labor but for the elegance of a polished style: are not such men rightly compared to sounding brass or a tinkling cymbal? Like tinkling brass or a cymbal they strive to speak great things rather than to do them, and they do not blush at their inconsistency in living otherwise than they preach. In order to obscure after a fashion the baseness of their way of life they do not cease to preach virtuous things—not, however, to help their listeners by their preaching, but to give themselves the appearance of practicing what they preach.

2. But let us see what the Apostle adds to this: *If*, he says, *I should have prophecy and should know all mysteries and all knowledge, and if I should have all faith so that I could remove mountains, and have not charity, I am nothing.*[53] He does not say this as if no one can have any virtues without charity; but he says it because those who possess virtues do not profit by them if they lack charity. Charity is indeed necessary here in order that all the virtues may avail those having the highest virtue, charity; and there it will abide even more perfectly in them when it has led to the sight of God all who have been faithful to it. Besides, prophecy and the knowing of all mysteries and knowledge and even faith itself

and the rest of such gifts,[54] which are considered necessary
not for the perfection of the faithful but for their frailty,
cannot be needful for those arriving at that perfection of the
saints which they, being rooted in charity, are striving to
attain, since incomparably better and more perfect things
will succeed them. For prophecy will not be needed there
because, being accomplished, it will have led to what it
promised; and there will be no need of knowledge, which
like a kind of lamp enlightens the faithful in the night of this
world, because in the perpetual day of that life the living
Sun [55] will shine upon the just; and the knowing of mysteries
and faith itself will not be necessary because Christian perfection will have arrived at what was signified by mystery and
believed by faith. But here, certainly, there is need of
charity, which separates us from the devil, purifies us from
sin, reconciles us to God; there, however, it will be perfect
when it has joined the perfect to God, by whom it was given.

3. The Apostle, still amplifying the praise of divine charity, adds: *If I should distribute my goods to feed the poor,
and if I should deliver my body to be burned, and have not
charity, it profiteth me nothing.*[56] And this is right; for, if
we are to be asked in that last examination not what we did
but why we did it, what will almsgiving or surrendering the
body to death profit us if we have not charity? We ought,
then, to seek and possess that virtue without which neither
almsgiving nor the killing of the body nor all those things
which were named above nor any other virtues whatsoever
lead any to salvation; for no good action or suffering unless
it springs from faith *that worketh by charity* [57] will be able
to help us. Wherefore, no damnable sin will be able to abide
and no good will be lacking in those who abound in charity,
the cleanser of all stain and the mother of all virtues. For

if, indeed, *charity is patient, is kind*; if it *envieth not, dealeth not perversely, is not puffed up, is not ambitious, seeketh not her own, is not provoked to anger, thinketh no evil, rejoiceth not in iniquity, but rejoiceth with the truth*; if it *beareth all things, believeth all things, hopeth all things, endureth all things*; [58] and if it imparts to those in whom it exists all the goods it possesses: who can be more perfect in this life than those who abound in so many virtues, charity reigning among them?

4. Accordingly, when we see that some men, established on the rock of patience, oppose stout hearts to raging evils; when we see them disposed by an abundance of holy benignity and wishing to share their possessions with everyone; not parched by any firebrands of burning envy; not doing any double-dealing but showing simple sincerity to all; not conceited by any arrogance of ruinous vanity; not contending for the possessions of others because of the crime of covetousness; not seeking their own before the common good; not scheming evil for anyone, by whatsoever injuries they are provoked; not rejoicing in anyone's iniquity or in the evil of their own works but in the truth; suffering all troublesome persons and all troubles with firm tranquillity of soul; when we see their faith in their fear of future punishments that are threatened by God; their joyous hope of promised rewards; their desire, expressed in their brave endurance, for the revelation of the sons of God; when, then, we see that some men can do these and similar good things, we may know that it is not by the greatness of their own virtue that they can accomplish what they ardently wish and what they do, but that it is by the help of that charity which is not of ourselves but which was *poured forth in our hearts by the Holy Ghost, who is given to us*. [59]

CHAPTER 15

The perfection conferred by charity on those established in it.

1. Accordingly, if we show charity to God and our neighbor *from a pure heart and a good conscience and an unfeigned faith,*[60] it becomes easy for us to resist sin, abound in all virtues, despise the allurements of the world, and accomplish even with delight all that is difficult or troublesome for human frailty; and this, provided that we love God with the perfect charity which we have from Him, with our whole heart, with our whole soul, and with all our strength.[61] For a man sins in that part in which he loves God less; if we love Him with our whole heart, there will be no part in us wherein we may serve the desires of sins. And what is it to love God except to be occupied with Him in our soul, to conceive the desire of enjoying the sight of Him, to have hatred of sin and contempt of the world, to love one's neighbor [62] also, whom He decreed should be loved in Himself, and in that love to observe a legitimate measure and not to pervert the established order of love? Those pervert the order of love and do not observe the measure of loving who either love the world, which ought to be despised; or love their bodies more, which they should love less; or do not love their neighbors as themselves; or perhaps do not love God more than themselves.[63]

2. But in regard to the world, which ought not to be loved at all, there is the statement of our God Himself made through the Apostle Saint John: *Love not the world.*[64] Our body, however, since it is part of us, we should love so that we may have regard, as nature ordains, for its health and frailty, and consider how it may, appointed as it is to be

subject to the spirit, attain eternal salvation and receive immortality and incorruptibility, and may not by yielding to its
passions weaken the strength of the soul yielding in turn to
it, nor mar its purity and corrupt all its dignity by the disease
of love for itself. As to our neighbors, we then love them as
ourselves when we love them not for any advantage to
ourselves, not for benefits expected or received,[65] not for
affinity or blood relationship, but for this reason alone that
they share our nature; for we do not love them as ourselves
when we love them for the reasons stated above. And, certainly, no one loves his neighbor as himself on this account,
that the person loved is his brother or sister, father or son,
mother or daughter, grandson or granddaughter. In fact, he
who so loves shows a carnal love, because not those alone
whom the bond of blood joins to us are to be considered our
neighbors; but we should think of all men as our neighbors
since they are sharers, as I have said, in our nature. For if
we love our kinsfolk, no matter how obstinate, base, and
unprincipled they are, more than holy individuals whom we
call strangers to us according to blood, not only do we love
carnally, but we even sin gravely by such a love for them.

3. Accordingly, we love all our neighbors as ourselves
when, in regard to morality and to gaining eternal life, we
have concern for their salvation as for our own; when we
imagine ourselves in their sins and dangers; and when, just
as we wish them to help us, so we come to their aid according
to our strength, or if we have not the means to help them,
have the will to do so. This, then, is the whole love of your
neighbor: the good you would like conferred on yourself you
wish also for him; and the evil you do not want to happen to
yourself you do not want to happen to him either.[66] Now,

those love God more than themselves who for love of Him do not spare their temporal welfare; who deliver themselves to tribulations and dangers; who are prepared to be stripped of their possessions, to be exiled, to renounce their parents and wives and children; and who, in fine, not only do not shrink from the very death of the body but even die gladly, desiring to give up the life of their body rather than God, the Life of their life.

4. This, then, is the order of love which we should maintain according to the word of the Holy Spirit, *He set in order charity in me*: [67] namely, that, as well-ordered charity demands, we should love God in the first place, and that for His sake we should love in Him, in as far as He ordains, that which we ought to love. For He commands us to love our bodies because of ourselves, our neighbors as ourselves, and God more than ourselves. But this is to be done in such a way that we devote ourselves more to those whom acquaintance brings in nearer connection with ourselves, provided their repute is not blameworthy and their way of life commends them, and that we regard the advancement of all as our own and grieve compassionately over the sins of others as over our own. Thus, then, can those who love God perfectly be perfect in this life; and they love Him perfectly who, by willing what He wills and by not willing what He does not will, do not consent to any sins, whereby He is offended, and always exert themselves to cherish and preserve the virtues which He deigns to bestow. These are they who sincerely believe that He gave them the power to accomplish all the good they have been able to do. Whatever evil they have committed they ascribe to the fault of their own will; whatever good they have not been able to accomplish they continu-

ally ask Him that they may be able; when they have been able, they thank Him. They charitably wish that His blessings, which they have attained, may be granted to others also; and, extending the breadth of their love even to their enemies, they wish all to be what they are.

Enough has been said of vices and their remedies. Now let me tell briefly how each virtue can be acquired.

CHAPTER 16

The nature of virtue; it permeates those of one mind with it.

1. Every holy virtue is a divine thing, without body and most pure. Unclean minds do not stain it; on the contrary, it purifies unclean minds. By sharing it shapeless things are given shape; dead things are raised up; sickness is cured; wrongs are righted; opposition is reconciled. Only God and he to whom God has given it possess it. It lives in the soul, but it sanctifies soul and body. No one acquires it against his will, no one loses it except when deceived by his own will. No one can give it to himself though he can take it away; on the other hand, he can neither give it to another nor take it from him.

2. Therefore, when a virtue of such greatness has shone upon anyone who up to that time has been languishing in his passions and has aroused in him a healthy longing to desire it, straightway a conflict of two contradictory desires arises in his soul, and his will draws his mind back and forth, divided against itself by a double love, now by abandoning what he had chosen, now by choosing what he had abandoned; and this lukewarm middle course, so to say, between

10 *

virtue and vice harasses and tortures him while he is driven this way and that by the diversity of his thoughts. For until a man by a strong determination confirms himself in what he has chosen —as long as he at one moment does not wish what he formerly wished; at another, begins to wish what he did not wish, as though placed in some crossroad [68] of indecision— that conflict of wills torments him. On one side virtue reminds him of his salvation and calls to him; on the other, vicious habit detains him when he wishes to withdraw from it and calls him back and by reminding him of his wonted pleasure tempts him, now that he has turned from it somewhat but has not been fully converted to virtue, and presents to him all the delights which he formerly basely enjoyed. It also instills in him evil desires which fetter him, and it seductively whispers some temptation to him, now almost disheartened, and it implores him not to prefer pain to pleasure, sorrow to joy, doubt to certainty, future enjoyment to present; to think how painful and difficult it is to be without sweet delights, to renounce carnal allurements, to be burdened by the hardships of continued abstinence, to be racked by endless fasts and vigils, to seek by a sure affliction of the flesh the prize of a doubtful reward, to take arms to resist the devil, who is skilled in deception; to avoid his tricks and deceits by the caution of a vigilant soul; to consider, finally, how wretched it is for one who has been overcome by the unreasonableness of so much austerity and deceived by a ruse of the devil to return to what he had foresworn, to enjoy the pleasure he had cast away, and to delight in all which he had spurned by imprudently undertaking a laborious way of life.

3. With these and similar arguments the habit of vice plagues one who is undecided in the presence of a holy

resolution. On the other hand, the virtue called temperance stoutly dissuades his hesitation and invites him to the pure pleasures and chaste delights which all its lovers enjoy. It offers him in his nakedness the garment of justice. It shows him, enlightened, the ornament of its own splendor. It promises him, distrustful of himself, the help of its protection. It encourages him and appeals to him to lay aside his indecision and to take up a spiritual way of life; to be confident that he will persevere in the execution of the resolution he has taken not by his own ability but by the mercy of the Lord; relying not on his own strength but on the help of all-powerful grace, to take up victorious arms against the devil's attacks; to consider how many men and women have been able and are able to do what he despairs of being able to do; to believe firmly that he will have the power from the same source from which they received it; with sure hope to prefer spiritual goods to carnal, heavenly to earthly, future to present.

CHAPTER 17

The rise of the converted to the height of perfection.

1. But when anyone, won by the convincing fairness of virtue, has broken to some extent with his former way of life, immediately there meets him another temptation against which he must struggle. For vanity of the world will attack the man whom carnal passion has abandoned in defeat, an example of which we have in those who deny themselves the enjoyment of lustful passion and allow their will the license of windy vanity. They have no intercourse with shame, but give in to ambition. They have a splendid table service and

garments carefully tailored to serve their ostentation, boys with neatly curled hair and powerful horses for their pageants, hawks and well-fed hounds for the hunt, frequent hunting parties to show their magnificence; they pretend that a display of gorgeous trappings is necessary ornature.

2. And, to laugh immoderately; to raise the voice in insolent hilarity; to be a ready listener to filthy jokes; to make the sorrow of others their own joy by causing them trouble; to heap gallantries on the fashionable, however vile they are; to disparage the worthy who lack the necessities of life; to build vast and magnificent homes; to increase their possessions without end; to brood over absorbing the property of others if opportunity offers: these things they regard as a matter not of covetousness but of some utility. Thus they not only deliberately do the things I have mentioned and many others like them but they even laugh at those who take them to task. They deem that persons who brand deeds lawful and customary for nobles with the charge of ambition, are talking nonsense. However, he who with the aid of God has conquered this vice also and, supported by the strength of spiritual temperance, has trampled on all that could keep him from perfection inclines his mind to holy virtue with the devotedness of a good will. Then he joyfully and faithfully obeys every nod of his sovereign, Queen Virtue, and so, being made one spirit with his God, he always does and thinks of nothing but that whereby he may become purer and nobler and may overcome the attractions of all the vices by pure delights.

CHAPTER 18

The perfection to be attributed to the number four; the four virtues called principal, being conferred by God, justify those who live by faith.

1. Let us now consider whether there is truth in the theory of the philosophers by which they establish four virtues as so many fountains of all virtues and also four vices as the sources of all evils. That the principal virtues number four, is not only held by the philosophers, but our own authorities are in agreement with them.[69] But why there are four and what are the works of each I ought to show briefly, the Lord enlightening me.

Practically everyone knows that the number four is consecrated to perfection.[70] Thus, the whole world is composed of four parts or corners: east and west, south and north; and the name of ADAM, who is the father of the human race, and the generic word HOMO are made up of four letters. The body also, being made up of four elements, contains in itself the mystery of the quaternary number. That there are also four emotions [71] of the soul itself, which we use either for good or for evil, even the ancients wisely discovered; and posterity has accepted and approved their conclusions.

2. The four rivers which flow from the fount of paradise,[72] the four Gospels, the four wheels of the divine chariot, and the four wings and four faces of the four animals [73] also abundantly commend the dignity of this number. And so we should carefully consider how much holiness these virtues, which contain so much perfection in their number, confer on

the Christian soul, and how no perfection exists anywhere which is not in these virtues. For, if temperance makes one temperate; prudence, prudent; justice, just; and fortitude, strong: I do not know what can be more perfect than he who acts temperately, prudently, justly, and strongly. And so it is indeed difficult to name the virtues which spring from the four which I have called principal virtues, though, when we begin to show their nature and works, perhaps from the very dispositions of each it will be apparent from which virtue each arises.

3. But this we should know and believe in the first place: these four virtues and all the virtues that spring from them are the gifts of God, and no one possesses them, did possess them, or will possess them unless God, who is the principle and source of all the virtues, has conferred them on him. For anyone who at any time in any nation lived by faith, believing in God, could surely by His gift become temperate and prudent, just and strong. On the contrary, those who, not knowing God or even blaspheming Him, have lived without faith are to be considered as not having the ability to receive any of these virtues from God or to possess them.

CHAPTER 19

The nature of temperance and the effect it produces.

1. But now let us see what is proper to each of the virtues. Temperance makes a man temperate, abstemious, frugal, sober, moderate, chaste, silent, serious, modest. Residing in the soul, this virtue bridles lust, tempers the affections, multiplies holy desires and represses corrupt ones, sets in order

all that is disordered within us, strengthens all that is well-ordered, removes wicked thoughts and implants holy ones, quenches the fire of lustful passion, kindles the tepidity of our soul by a desire of future reward, soothes our mind with peaceful tranquillity, and ever preserves it intact from every storm of vices. Temperance reduces our intemperance in food and drink to just limits so that we are content with what is placed before us; so that we do not brazenly ask for what our host perhaps does not have; do not offend others by what appeals to our desires; do not let the intemperate craving of our appetite appear; do not criticize those who prefer to abstain from foods which we eat or embarrass those who perchance eat those things from which we abstain and thank God for them, since we realize that it is a very wretched thing to condemn others for taking food or drink or to lay claim to sanctity because of our abstinence.

2. By temperance we reverence our elders; honor our equals fraternally; give the favor of paternal love to our juniors. We are silent when an older person is talking; wait for him to signal us to speak; do not lift our voices immoderately in conversation; do not allow our laughter to break out into rude hilarity; do not detract anyone or bear calmly with detractors, realizing that both detractors and those who agree with them are corrupted by the passion of vanity. Such persons wish others to seem vile so that they may praise themselves by comparison with those they criticize and may seem not to have those vices which they maliciously reprove in others. This evil temperance removes; he who wishes to serve it looks not for what he may censure in his brethren but for a reason to praise God. And it is accordingly characteristic of this temperance not only that we are temperate in the use

of all our members but also that we willingly do all the things that make us moderate and sober. But let these words about temperance suffice so that I may also discuss fortitude.

CHAPTER 20

The type of persons ennobled by fortitude of soul.

1. That should be counted as fortitude of soul which not only remains unshaken when attacked by diverse troubles but also does not weaken and succumb to any enticements of pleasure. But if the soul really breaks the attacks of raging evils; if it resists whatever calamities assail it; if it continues untired amid the harshness of the assaults made upon it, amid the blasts of pressing anxieties, amid enmities and perils and persecutions of many kinds, and yet boasts of resisting its enemies by its own power and exults not in the gift of God, whereby it is enlightened, but delights carnally in the favor of the crowd which praises it; and if it rejoices more for being praised than for having reason to be praised, and therefore prefers human praise to the divine gifts: who doubts that this disposition of soul cannot be called virtue? If it were virtue, it would stoutly resist such temptations also; nor would it give in to soft things when with the help of the Lord it had overcome hard and difficult things. Yes, there are people whom covetousness of the world makes impervious to strong passions; but here one should not praise their self-control but marvel at their insensibility.[74]

2. Those whom love of God renders strong to bear their sufferings, no delight of the flesh, no enticement of evil passions can corrupt because, if not what we suffer but why

we suffer is the important thing, patience does not reside in those who bear distress calmly, but only in those whom justice has caused to bear it strongly. Accordingly, the Lord did not say: *Blessed are they that suffer persecution*, and hold His peace; but He added: *for justice' sake*,[75] in order that He might clearly show that not suffering but motive constitutes true patience; and so He promised happiness not to those suffering persecution but to those suffering it *for justice' sake*. If this is so, endurance of evils that must be overcome is then true patience if it is just; and patience is just in those whose insuperable determination yields neither to sorrows nor to pleasures. But we have this fortitude of soul from Him whom we praise with the Prophet: *The Lord is my strength and my praise; and He is become my salvation*.[76] He is our strength because by His invincible protection He so strengthens us against all the vices that prosperity does not enervate our soul nor does adversity cast it down. And then does the Lord become our praise when we wish men not to praise us because of God's gifts, but to praise His gifts in us. Those whose salvation the Lord has become cannot boast of their own virtue.

3. Let him, then, whose strength of soul is the Lord yield to no carnal desires, give in to no passions; let him conquer ambition and the esteem of the crowd. Let not the love of money enslave him; let not the anguish caused by sufferings and losses cast him down. Let God be his whole praise, perfect glory, pure delight, sure hope, firm security, unimpaired strength, incorrupt health, so that whatever in this world pleases the carnal may displease him; whatever seems precious may become worthless; whatever appears brilliant may pale in contemplation of things to come. Let him

not permit himself to be strangled by what he has already strangled by God's grace. It certainly seems all the more shameful for his soul to be overcome by the vices he has overcome; and it profits him nothing to have overcome some of his vices if he becomes subject to one he has neglected to master. For not that man is wont to be considered strong who distinguishes himself by undertaking labors and dangers or who begins to bridle and rule his passions; but he should be regarded great and noble, valiant and worthy of the name of fortitude, who permits no vice to renew war on him or to conquer him. Only let faintheartedness not be present lest we despair of being able to do what we can do; let there be no vicious presumption lest we ascribe to ourselves what we are able to do only by the grace of God. For, whether we despair of God's gift whereby we are strengthened, or boast of our own ability, we are not equal to the task of resisting vices. At all events, fortitude of soul should drive out the cowardice of despair as well as overcome boasting.

CHAPTER 21

Justice and, proceeding from it, faith.

Up to this point I have discussed the virtue called fortitude. Now let us see what assistance justice also affords us in this life and how it, too, cannot be overcome by any attacks of vices in the hearts of those who have given themselves over to it. For faith, which is the foundation of justice,[77] which no good works precede and from which they all proceed, cleanses us from all sins, enlightens our minds, conciliates us to God, and unites us with all who share our nature. It inspires us with the hope of future reward, increases holy virtues in us, and confirms us in their possession.

CHAPTER 22

Equity; the advancement of human society is its concern.

From justice equity also flows, which makes us call the necessities of all men our own and makes us believe we were born not for ourselves alone but also for mankind in general. It makes us avoid whatever can harm any man as though it were to harm ourselves; for we who are men should think nothing human alien to us.[78] Of beasts it is of course characteristic to live for themselves and not to share their advantages.[79] We differ from them not only by the gift of intelligence but also by respect for the equality of law if, looking on the advantage or disadvantage of others as on our own, we live for the benefit of all who share our nature. Furthermore, if it is the nature of wild animals to attack, to wound or kill one another, who doubts that it accords with human excellence for men to aid, teach, and edify one another, and to care for the advantage of all as for their own? From this it may be understood that those who, though they were born human, persist in oppressing and deceiving their fellow men, degenerate into the habits of wild beasts by a change not of their nature but of their manner of life.

CHAPTER 23

The two kinds of injustice.

1. There are two kinds of injustice: one, whereby we inflict injuries; the other, whereby we neglect to avert those inflicted by others when we can. For in a certain sense we ourselves are oppressors when we scorn the downtrodden

though we are able to defend them from oppression. Nor does it avail me anything that I do not circumvent or deceive a man if I permit him to be deceived or circumvented. This same thing may be understood of sins; for, if I see a man commit a sin and I not only do not reprove him but even consent to his sin, I make myself a sharer in his damnation; and I sin in all who sin when, because of a certain malice in my unfeeling soul, I do not censure those who I know have sinned or are sinning.

2. And, certainly, we should not listen to those who say they cannot reprove sinners for the reason that they do not wish to make enemies of persons who are unwilling to correct themselves. While they are careful of the good will of their brethren, these men are careless of their salvation. But if we reprove not out of pride but out of mercy and with a certain compassion of a sympathetic soul, and if they feel that we are moved not less by their sins than by our own, either they, being changed for the good, give thanks to God with us; or if the attraction of sinning still keeps them in sin, and if, seeing that we are concerned for their salvation, they wish to return evil for good, we should prefer to incur the enmity of those who are unwilling to be corrected rather than to risk offending God by humoring sinners. However, since I have already said much about these things in the second book,[80] let me finish treating the other aspects of justice as I began.

CHAPTER 24

Generosity and the practice of beneficence.

1. From the fountain of justice there also proceed generosity, beneficence, charity, and the rest of such virtues where-

by men can be helped in many ways. It is generosity which overflows even upon those who seem to lack nothing; on this generosity the surplus of domestic goods is spent.

The works of beneficence are many, which mercifully relieve the need of the afflicted and purchase an inheritance of the heavenly kingdom with earthly wealth, provided only that the benefaction is done without any ostentation and that the unseemly love of popular esteem is not our inducement to exercise compassion. Some are to be found who, it is true, help the various necessities of different persons; but they are motivated by the desire of acquiring a reputation, or they are moved by carnal pity, or they are constrained by the hope of receiving back what they give or by the need of making a return for what they have received.

2. There are others whom shrewd covetousness alone prompts to give anything to the poor. Their purpose in bestowing certain things is that in this life they may receive greater things. And whatever has been given them as pastors of the poor to spend on the needy, for whose sustenance they have received it, they spend entirely, or almost entirely, on their own pleasures; and—what is worse—they shamefully crave to be counted among the generous and compassionate or even to be praised above them. Utterly different from all these and their kind are those who wish not themselves, but God, to be praised in their deeds. They are led to good work by the hope of future recompense and wish to have as witness of their labor Him alone from whom they believe with all the fibers of their faith that they will receive their reward.

CHAPTER 25

The different kinds of love; perfect love as distinguished from them.

Now, then, because the subject requires it, I shall also note a few things here about charity, of which I have already said much in this book. I say nothing of carnal love, which, beginning in marriage, extends unto children; for such love we have in common with cattle and beasts. I pass over love of relatives also, because evidently this, too, still pertains to flesh and blood. Nor do I say anything of the love which, though we love our friends according to it, is, nevertheless, also referable to some temporal advantage. Not that these loves are not honorable since they are natural to all; but the love wherewith we freely love God and our friend is incomparably superior. But he who loves his friend for any profit proves that he loves not his friend but his own advantage. And, indeed, he who loves a person for any temporal thing will cease to love him when the object, inasmuch as it is temporal, ceases to exist. But one who loves for the sake of God—just as God is eternal, so that love for his friend will remain forever. And, accordingly, because there is no greater or better object of love than God, love for Him is perfect love. If, however, He is loved at all for His gifts, He is surely not loved freely since then that for which He is loved is placed above Him—a thing which it is wicked even to say. But for all His lovers He Himself is their blessed life and eternal salvation and everlasting kingdom and joy. These, they who love God will receive; for He alone will be all things to them when *He will be all in all.*[81]

CHAPTER 26

Giving each man his due.

Therefore, if in this life we are trying to fulfill justice, whose work it is to render each man his due, let us give ourselves back to God by whom we were made, and let us not permit ourselves to be dominated by those things over which we have been placed in command according to our nature. Let reason master the vices; let the body be subject to the soul and the soul to God; and the whole perfection of man is accomplished. And so, we, too, being made sharers in justice, render each man his due if we neglect inferior things for better ones, and carnal delights for virtues; and just as in reasoning we prefer living things to non-living, sentient to living, intelligent to sentient, immortal to mortal, so by living well let us prefer useful things to those things that give pleasure, the honorable to the useful, the holy to the honorable, and perfection to holiness. But the body will not be able to conform to the spirit, nor the appetite to reason, unless God, who created that spirit and body, being pleased with our thoughts, rests in us and works in our heart like a true tiller of the soil [82] in his field, so that whatever faith plants in it and devotion waters He Himself may bring to the increase of perfect maturity and may so subdue our evil desires, when we have become subject to Him of our own accord, that from our very works it may be apparent who dwells in us [83] and whose will is done in us.

CHAPTER 27

Three virtues—temperance, fortitude, and justice—perfect the active life. Prudence, which is the fourth virtue, furnishes the mind knowledge of hidden things.

This is the order of nature and of justice. He who is careful to hold and observe it will fulfill the perfection of the active life. For this active life those three virtues, of which I have said by request, God granting, what I believed should be said, are helpful; for temperance and fortitude of soul and justice constitute spiritual action, without which that knowledge which seems to pertain to prudence is of no avail, since it will profit us nothing to have learned what we should do unless we strive to carry out what we have learned.

The capacity of the soul, then, which is divided into appetite and reason, is helped to attain the perfection of a good act and to gain knowledge of hidden things by these four virtues on which I have already dwelt at some length. By three of them: that is, temperance and fortitude of soul and justice, the appetite itself is formed so that an act may be done; prudence, on the other hand, enlightens reason, which is the eye of the mind, so that reason may govern the appetite and the appetite submit to reason. For every virtue, as the ancients put it, consists in just three things: one is in examining in each case what is true and sincere—the proper office of prudence, which I shall treat in its own place; the second, in restraining and tempering the disordered emotions of the soul, which the Greeks call *páthē*,[84] so that all inclinations, which the Greeks call *hormaí*,[85] are made subject to reason; the third, in wishing to use those with whom we are associated so as to gain the fullness of their salvation and our own. All these are seen to belong to the work of the other three virtues; among them temperance and fortitude are particularly strong in restraining and bridling the disturbances of the soul which many call passions, others, infirmities.[86] When these have been tempered and put in order according to a certain formula of temperance and fortitude, all virtues without any contradictions of vices reign in the man who is subject to his Creator.

CHAPTER 28

The social virtue. Those do wrong who do not help human society when they can.

1. Now, justice, whereby those who have practiced it become just, is regarded as something of a social virtue because it grows with the kindness it shows others. For who does not himself profit by that very thing whereby he wishes another to profit? Who does not make God compassionate to himself when he has shown himself compassionate towards the afflicted or erring? Or how will he not increase all his goodness in himself who not only does not envy those who have possessions but, in as far as he can, by the inspiration of God even shares his goods with those who have no possessions?

In view of this one should consider whether they act justly who, removing themselves from all occupations and devoting themselves to spiritual pursuits, do nothing for human society and, preferring their own desires to the advantage of all, disregard the common good by choosing a welcome freedom. For, to be unwilling to help the afflicted when you can, to wish to enjoy restful quiet without regard for the common good is surely not equity. Those who respect this equity all live for the good of all and, as though born for one another, guard and love one another's salvation. And, consequently, they act contrary to justice who, when they have been chosen because of the merit of their way of life or their learning, give preference to leisurely study over the fruitful good of ruling the common folk and who, though they could help the Church in its labors, shun the work of a burdensome administration for the sake of enjoying repose.

2. But since there are many who realize that they are unequal to so great a responsibility, such men rightly do not accept it even when they are pressed lest they appear to wish not to undertake labors for the Church but to seek honors, whereas ecclesiastical dignity should be neither sought nor refused.[87] If those who really can command people and be useful to them have not been asked, rightly do they give themselves to study to gain wisdom. But if administrators, who prosper through those who make progress because of them, and if scholars, who advance by themselves under God by acquiring spiritual wisdom, remain in their chosen way of life, they proceed by different roads, it is true, but they travel towards one homeland and arrive at one kingdom, doing service in different capacities as Christ, the King of all,[88] calls them. For who does not know that as studious leisure fills the man who is free from carnal affairs with the ineffable sweetness of heavenly wisdom, so the spiritual occupation of holy labors brings manifold fruits to him who is taken up with the good of human society? In those spiritual studies, too, who can sufficiently estimate how much ecclesiastical men can profit since by teaching their inferiors they

exercise themselves; and by conferring with those equally learned they become more careful in many things; and by listening to those who are more learned they renounce opinions they had imprudently formed, hold right opinions more firmly, understand mysteries, and reach decisions in those matters about which they were fluctuating in doubt? But since the plan of my discussion requires me to say a few things also concerning prudence, the fourth cardinal virtue, let what I have said of justice suffice.

CHAPTER 29

*From the fount of prudence and wisdom those who are
eagerly intent on gaining learning drink knowledge
of all things.*

1. Prudence and wisdom are generally associated with the investigation and discovery of truth. With that in view, I think that he cannot rightly be called wise who has not prudence, nor can he be called prudent who has not wisdom. Wherefore, if the work of prudence and wisdom is regarded as nothing but the investigation and discovery of truth, he who can prudently seek the truth and wisely find it will rightly be called prudent and wise. This I would say first, in order that whatever will be said of prudence can in its entirety be understood as having been said of wisdom also, because these two virtues are so connected and united and so little can either of them exist without the other that what is imprudent cannot be called wisdom, and what is unwise cannot be called prudence. Now, if the whole perfection of human life consists in action and in knowledge, just as I have proved that action is perfected by the union of temperance and fortitude

and justice, so let me prove that knowledge of things comes from the acquisition of prudence.

2. Knowledge of things, proceeding as it does from the fountain of prudence and wisdom, enlightens all spiritual persons who have cleansed themselves of carnal vices and inflames those who have turned from all pleasure in harmful curiosity to the desire of contemplating virtue, with these results: by gaining knowledge of divine and human things they become truly prudent and wise; they foresee and at the same time guard against [89] evils which threaten them; and they realize that there are no evil things except those which make men evil. No passions banish any part of their moderation or tranquillity since they are, so to speak, unconscious of them. They distinguish between false and real goodness. They prudently hold that nothing in this world occurs by chance or without justice, but that everything happens through God, who wills and permits it; those who think differently they either wisely teach or reprove. They understand that the various sorrows and diverse weaknesses which afflict men subject to death do not always follow from sins that have preceded but often happen to those born in corruption from the very nature of their mortality; and, knowing that they are not condemned but that they are proved by present adversities,[90] acting manfully, they seize the opportunity from that bearing of sorrows to gain patience; they do not harm others or allow themselves to be harmed.

3. Such the Lord in the Gospel commands us to become, saying: *Be ye wise as serpents and simple as doves;* [91] for the simple cannot circumvent anyone, nor do the prudent permit themselves to be circumvented. But if in any contract or in a conversation or in anything else one does not let himself

be deceived and yet deceives another, such a man does not have prudence, which is the cause of salvation rather than of perdition, but he pretends to have it; for virtue differs from vice precisely in this: the latter corrupts sound things; the former heals what the attack of vice had corrupted. And thus, a really prudent man is eager to help all whom he can in order that he may increase his fruits by the merits of all who are won to God through him. But if he plans anyone's damnation or rejoices over the fate of one who perishes, a man necessarily perishes himself before he causes another to be lost; and the perdition which he wishes to another begins with his own ruin.

CHAPTER 30

The prudent neither harm others nor permit themselves to be harmed. They will have consummate prudence without any admixture of error there where life will be perfect without any sin.

1. As I was saying, those who, being made prudent by sharing in prudence, approach their God—not by walking but by living in a holy manner—in the degree to which they are prudent by the gift of God, cannot perish through either their own sin or another's; but since their prudence is not yet so perfect as it will be in that life wherein no error at all can overtake those who live perfectly, even prudent men sometimes yield to deceptive sins. These men are not depraved in will but, being human, they fall through human error. Nor are they at this time made perfect by the complete attainment of prudence and wisdom as they will be there where they can no longer be ignorant of anything and can no longer commit sin.

2. But if here below a good deed could have been discerned perfectly from an evil deed, never would he pray to be cleansed from his secret sins who says: *From my secret ones cleanse me, O Lord; and from those of others spare Thy servant.*[92] In these words he makes it clear enough that even those who live holy lives through the gift of the Holy Spirit, nevertheless, because of some frailties which they bear, knowingly or unknowingly either fall at times into sin or consent to another's sin. In this life, then, where sin is committed by will or by error or by weakness,[93] those who with the help of God do not sin voluntarily actually live above reproach. But because error or weakness can involve them in sins, they trustingly ask Him to enlighten and cure them who was called on exultingly in the Spirit by the man who said: *The Lord is my light and my salvation; whom shall I fear?*[94] Thus, when the light bestowed by the gift of prudence and wisdom has taken away blindness and when salvation, infused by the grace of God, has cured our weakness, then the mind, being divinely illuminated and healed, is not deceived by human error in regard to those things it should avoid or seek so as either to defend error for truth or to reject truth for error; and it is able without any hindrance of weakness to effect the good it has chosen.

3. Yet the salvation of this life whereby one lives mortally is one thing; the salvation of that life where our mortality will be granted immortality is another. In the present life we have been saved in hope; in the other we shall be saved in reality. Here our salvation is such that we still can perish; there whoever has been saved will no longer be able to perish. And so, the knowledge which affords us an understanding of things while living in the night of this world is to be

considered, when compared to its future fullness, as a part of knowledge, not the whole. For this reason the holy Apostle says: *For we know in part, and we prophesy in part. But when that which is perfect is come, that which is in part shall be done away.*[95] He declares that it will be done away, that is, consummated, because the part of knowledge which is to be perfected is really not to be done away, but it is to be made full by the perfect. Accordingly, in that place where there will be perfect salvation of all faithful Catholics, where there will be incorruptibility and blessed immortality, there the true perfection of prudence and wisdom and the entire understanding of all things will exist because knowledge will have been brought to perfection by the doing away with the part.

CHAPTER 31

The four emotions. These should not be counted among the vices if their use proceeds from a good will.

1. Let us now see what careful study may discover about the four emotions also, which the stupidity of the worldly wise [96] regards as vices. For if only sinners or the wicked could at all fear and grieve, desire and rejoice, rightly could some of these emotions be called not dispositions but disorders. Since, however, such impulses of the soul are found in the holy Apostles and Prophets, who would be so foolish as to regard as vices those emotions whereby those who more than the rest of men resisted vices pleased God? Accordingly, the Apostle Paul speaks of fear in these terms: *But I fear lest, as the serpent seduced Eve by his subtilty, so also your minds should be corrupted . . . from the innocence that is in Christ.*[97] Likewise, of desire he confidently says: *I desire to*

be dissolved and to be with Christ.[98] And of sadness, too, which others call sorrow, the same vessel of election and teacher of the Gentiles [99] says: *That I have great sadness and continual sorrow in my heart . . . for my brethren, who are my kinsmen according to the flesh.*[100] And of joy also, after saying in writing to the Romans: *Your obedience is published in every place,* he says, *I rejoice in you; but I would have you to be wise in good and simple in evil.*[101] He who wishes to criticize this fear or this sorrow, this desire, this joy, criticizes the Apostle himself, who not only pleased God by such emotions but even reproved certain men as guilty because they were *without affection.*[102] And the Prophet, too, in saying: *I rejoiced at the things that were said to me,*[103] and, in the person of our Lord: *I looked for one that would grieve together with me, but there was none,*[104] commends such joy and sadness. And when another says: *The fear of the Lord driveth out sin,*[105] and: *The desire of wisdom bringeth to the kingdom,*[106] he not only does not censure but even praises the emotion of spiritual desire and fear of the Lord.

2. Not by having these emotions, then, but by using them badly, do we transgress. For the nature of human emotions indicates the Creator of man; their quality shows man's good or bad will.[107] And so, these same impulses which are emotions in men become virtues in those who use them well and passions or agitations or, as some like to say, disorders in those who lead evil lives.[108] Nor should we listen to the Stoics,[109] who contend that these emotions can and should be utterly eradicated because there is no sensation at all where no impulse of fear or of sorrow, of desire or of joy is found. Then, as though they regretted their own proposition, making

an exception of sadness, which they say does not befall the soul of the wise man, they declare that the other emotions, with change of name, do exist in the wise. They say *caution* instead of *fear*; *happiness* instead of *joy*; and *wish* instead of *desire*—as if a wise man does not fear, yet takes precautions; or wishes, yet does not desire; or does not rejoice in this life, yet is happy. They do not, however, believe that his soul grieves since sadness, which usually comes from the commission of sin, cannot by any remembrance of sin trouble the wise man, who they think commits no sin. That this reasoning is utterly without foundation, our Lord, born according to the flesh, shows; for He both sorrowed and wept.[110] Yet this sadness wherewith He was sad did not come to Him from His own sins since He who was conceived and born without sin not only did not sin but also could not sin.[111]

3. However, in order that those who think that a wise man cannot be sad or sorrowful may be refuted by their own authors, too, let them read what their most learned writer says: " For not to grieve at all is achieved not without paying a high price of callousness in the soul and of insensibility in the body." [112] But as to fear, which they consider an evil, our Scripture says: *The fear of the Lord is holy, enduring for ever and ever.*[113] However, we must properly confess that this fear is different from that other penal fear of which the Apostle says: *Fear is not in charity; but perfect charity casteth out fear;* [114] for the latter fear deters from evil those who wish to sin and holds them in good against their will; but the former fear, of which the Prophet says: *He that is without fear cannot be justified,*[115] grows the more with the increase of charity; and it is one thing for a man to fear lest he incur an evil for which he may be punished; it is another,

to fear lest he lose a good whereby he is delighted. Not all fear, then, should be regarded as a vice, but only that of which it is written: *Because fear hath pain.*[116] On the other hand, that fear of which it is said: *The fear of the Lord driveth out sin,* and: *He that is without sin cannot be justified,* and: *The fear of the Lord is holy, enduring for ever and ever,* should not be counted among the vices but should rather be considered as an enemy of the vices.

4. Now, when they say: " The good will; the bad desire "; or, " The good are happy; the evil rejoice," who of sound mind would admit these distinctions? Nay, who in his right mind would not refute them? For our Scripture reproves the man of evil will, saying: *Be not willing to make any manner of lie;*[117] and Tullius, the orator of greatest renown, counts desire as a good when he says: " I desire, conscript fathers, to be forbearing ";[118] and one among their group, Vergil, disparages happiness, saying:

Thence they fear and desire, grieve and are happy;[119]

for he counted the happiness of an evil mind as evil. And among us joy is counted as a good, as the Prophet says: *Be glad in the Lord and rejoice, ye just.*[120]

5. And so, without any unnecessary distinction of the Stoics, all the just and those perfected by entire holiness of morals fear and take precaution, will and desire, rejoice and are happy, sorrow and grieve. It makes a great difference, though, what they fear or shun, take precautions about, will, or desire; why they rejoice or are happy, sorrow or grieve. They fear to lose the inheritance of the celestial kingdom; they desire to reach their heavenly homeland. They grieve when tempted; they rejoice when freed from temptation. And thus, a right mind has right emotions; a wicked mind, wicked emotions.[121]

6. The holy bishop Augustine, keen in mind, charming in eloquence, skilled in human learning, zealous in ecclesiastical labors, celebrated in daily disputations, self-possessed in his every action, Catholic in his exposition of our faith, penetrating in the solution of problems, prudent in the refutation of heretics, and wise in explaining the canonical writings [122] —he, I say, whom I have followed in these little books to the best of my ability, in this manner settles the question I am treating, saying: " If these impulses, these emotions, which come from a love of good and from holy charity, are to be called vices, let us allow that what are real vices are called virtues. But since these emotions follow right reason when they are used as they should be, who would then dare to call them diseases and vicious passions? " [123] In order to show that these emotions are in us from the condition of our mortality and that they are necessary for this life, not for the future life, the same doctor adds a little farther on: " But though we have these emotions rightly and according to God, they belong to this life, not to that which we hope will be." [124]

CHAPTER 32

These emotions, without which there is no right living in this life, will not exist in that future happiness, which will have in store neither fear nor sorrow.

And so, if these emotions were not in us by reason of our infirmity, never would we yield for long to them by sorrowing or weeping against our will. But we feel that they are necessary for this life because in this mortality we cannot live at all rightly without them. For, if one does not fear or beware as long as he lives mortally lest he himself or another, whom he loves in Christ, lose his faith; if he is not saddened or does not grieve over his own sins or his neighbor's; if he neither rejoices nor shows happiness over progress; if he does not wish for or desire virtue: not only does he not live rightly but he even loses the feeling of humanity itself. In that blessed life, however, where all corruptibility and mortality will be blotted out and they will arrive who are to be there, where there can be neither tears nor sighs, there all the saints will have perfect love, no fear, and everlasting joy. There they will have a right will and no desire; for by enjoying the celestial blessings which they longed to attain they will lack nothing which they might further desire; and in that region of everlasting security and perfect peace and happiness they will not suffer the pangs of fear or sorrow. Fear, however— not that fear which *charity casteth out* [125] but that which charity fosters—perchance will endure for ever and ever [126] because those things to which that fear has led will endure for ever and ever.

CHAPTER 33

The four virtues called principal virtues both defend as from
sin in the present life and will remain with us
forever to the exclusion of every sin.

1. But although those four virtues of which I have spoken briefly will exist there, they will, nevertheless, be present [127] in a way far different from that of this life where they are in incessant conflict with vices and where, because of the uncertain outcome of the undecided struggle, they sometimes abandon the negligent who are unwilling to hearken to them, and again through the mercy of God go over to or return to others who repent of their sins. For, although tem-

perance will exist there, it will not be in order to check or vanquish evil desires or vices but in order to perfect those whom it here defended from the assault of intemperance, with the result that the blessed reception of their reward will completely satisfy them, made perfect in every part.

2. There, too, fortitude of soul will exist, not in order to repel any evils or to sustain them calmly but to maintain the blessed firmly in their eternal goodness without any evils. There perfect justice will exist in all the perfect, not in order to maintain a distinction between virtues and vices, for the bodies themselves will no longer be subject to vice, but in order to confer everlasting rewards on the perfect. This will then happen when through the destruction of all carnal concupiscence the spirit will not lust against the flesh nor the flesh against the spirit,[128] but the soul, subject to God, will reign in everlasting peace with the flesh subject to it and will cling happily to its Creator forever.

Now, as to prudence, which is regarded great even here where it enlightens prudent men *in* some *dark manner*,[129] what will it be there where without any deceiving figures it will show the truth to the perfect whom here the search of truth delighted? There the perfect, being divinely enlightened by receiving the fullness of prudence and wisdom, will without any hindrance of corruptibility and mortality know all they here desired to know perfectly and could not know; and they will contemplate not only the nature of all created things but also the very majesty of their Creator with face unveiled.

CHAPTER 34

The writer offers an apology for his whole work.

1. And so, with your leave, let this book also come to a close; otherwise, if it is unduly drawn out, it may displease not only because of its wretchedness but also because of its excessive wordiness. This, however, I entreat and beg of all who may chance to read it: to ascribe to the fault of my incompetence whatsoever they find worthy of blame in the matter itself, which I have treated as I could, and condescendingly to make allowance for me since, in my desire to obey the one who charged me with this, I presumed to take up a task quite exceeding my strength. But that which they approve as having been said conformably to the Catholic faith, let them attribute to God, *who giveth to all men abundantly and upbraideth not;* [130] and for all those things may they give thanks with me.

2. For the rest, the niceties of an elegant style are not a concern to me; nor am I ashamed if my discussion, which perhaps meets approval in regard to subject matter, offends some lovers of empty words by the rudeness of its uncultivated language; for I could not employ in my discourse what I did not acquire by studying with a learned master.[131] And yet, since a consciously elaborated style weakens the vital force of ideas and since studied brilliance drains all the vigor of what is said, who would not judge that I was right to disregard the desire to write something striking even if I could have attained it, like a man accomplished in speaking? Wherefore, I considered that composition adequate for my task which would bring out mental concepts with a measure

of indispensable clarity, not that which would serve to fascinate the ears. For, if I am not mistaken, a good Latin style is one that expresses briefly and clearly the things to be understood—provided of course that the proper signification of ordinary words is observed—not one that luxuriates in the beauteous charm of flowery eloquence.[132] Besides, the prudent-minded are pleased not by the ornamental but by the forceful; for things have not been provided for the sake of words, but words have been devised to express things.[133]

NOTES

INTRODUCTION

[1] Cf. C. F. Arnold, *Caesarius von Arelate und die gallische Kirche seiner Zeit* (Leipzig 1894) 84.

[2] *Ibid.* 83. Of course, the history of pastoral instruction and theology in the West before Pomerius includes such illustrious names as St. Ambrose (*De officiis ministrorum*), St. Jerome (*Ad Nepotianum, Ad Heliodorum, Ad Rusticum*), and above all St. Augustine (*De catechizandis rudibus, De doctrina Christiana*), whom Pomerius confesses (3. 31. 5) to have followed throughout as his guide.

[3] Isidore, *De vir. ill.* 25. 31 (ML 83. 1096A) alone uses the name Julianus. H. Howitt in his English translation of the 1930 edition of Cayré's *Précis de patrologie et d'histoire de la théologie* employs the spelling Pomarus.

[4] Cf. E. Norden, *Die antike Kunstprosa* (Leipzig 1923) 631-42: " Der neue Stil—Gallien."

[5] The chief sources are Isidore, *loc. cit.*, and the continuator of Gennadius, *De vir. ill.* 98 Richardson.

[6] Arnold, *op. cit.*, 82, suggests that Pomerius' change of residence may have been caused by the persecution of the African Church by the Vandals. If this is so, the probable date is before 484, since Gunthamund's tolerant rule began in that year.

[7] *Vita S. Caesarii Episcopi* 1. 8 (ML 67. 1004 f.). In this early biography, as well as often in the sermons of St. Caesarius, one finds echoes of Pomerius' teaching as expressed in the *De vita contemplativa*; cf. Arnold, *op. cit.* 122-28. For Pomerius' influence in determining the interest and respect shown by St. Caesarius for the writings of St. Augustine, and, indirectly, the justification of the Doctor of Grace in Gaul, cf. Arnold, 83 f., 115 ff., 125; also A. Malnory, *Saint Césaire, évêque d'Arles* (Paris 1894) 23. For a critical estimate of the work of Malnory and Arnold, see P. Lejay, " Césaire," *Dict. de théol. cath.* 2. 2 (1932) 2185.

[8] Ps.-Gennadius, loc. cit.

[9] Ruricius, *Ep.* 1. 17, 2. 10 (CSEL 21. 369 f., 385 f.).

[10] Arnold, *op. cit.* 82, thinks that prior to his coming to Gaul Pomerius had been at the head of some monastery in Africa. D.

Mangeant in his *Admonitio* to the treatise (reprinted in ML 59. 411-15) suggests that Pomerius may have been in charge of the same monastery which St. Caesarius later governed (from *ca.* 499 to *ca.* 503), before his elevation to the episcopacy of Arles; cf. M. Chaillan, *S. Césaire* (Paris 1921) 30. This would place Pomerius' death in *ca.* 499, for the *Vita S. Caesarii Episcopi* (1. 11) says expressly that Caesarius was chosen in the place of the *dead* abbot. Regarding this suggestion, see Arnold, *op. cit.* 92; also below, n. 13.

[11] Notably 2. 10. 2; 2. 16 and 17; 3. 28. Cf. O. Bardenhewer, *Geschichte der altkirchlichen Literatur* 4 (Freiburg i. Br. 1924) 599.

[12] Cf. above, n. 9.

[13] It is hardly likely that Ruricius would have tried to persuade a man who was in charge of a monastery to desert the establishment over which he had been placed.

[13a] Ruricius, *Ep.* 2. 9 (CSEL 21. 385).

[14] Ennodius, *Ep.* 2. 6 (CSEL 6. 44). This invitation must be dated not earlier than 493, the year in which Ennodius received orders.

[15] *Loc. cit.*

[16] Summaries of the eight books of this treatise are given by Isidore and the continuator of Gennadius (cf. above, nn. 3 and 5). Isidore remarks that in Book 2 of the *De Anima* Pomerius argues for the corporeality of the soul. Since Faustus of Riez (+ 490-500) had revived the error of Tertullian and had spread it with considerable success, the imputation is likely.

[17] *De vita contemplativa* 3. 31. 6.

[18] Chrodegang is the author of a rule which provided for community life, *vita canonica*, among the secular clergy of his see. In it he quotes from the *De vita contemplativa*, ascribing it to Prosper (Mansi 14. 328).

[19] It is exploited or quoted at some length by Paulinus of Aquileia (+ 802) in his *Liber exhortationis* (ML 99. 197-282); Halitgar of Cambrai (+ *ca.* 830), *De vitiis et virtutibus* (ML 105. 657-78); and by Jonas of Orleans (+ *ca.* 843) in *De institutione laicali* (ML 106. 121-278). It is used more briefly by Theodulphus of Orleans (+ 821) in his treatise *De Spiritu Sancto* (ML 105. 259-76); Rhabanus Maurus (+ 856), *Tractatus de anima* (ML 110. 1109-120); and by Atto of Vercelli in his (*ca.* 940) *De pressuris ecclesiasticis* (ML 134. 82-93). The *De vita contemplativa* appears also in the records of synods at Aix-la-Chapelle (817) and Paris (829); cf. Mansi 14. 231 and 540. In subsequent ages writers continued to regard St. Prosper as its

author. Cf. R. Ceillier, *Histoire générale des auteurs sacrés et ecclésiastiques* 15 (Paris 1748) 452 f.

[20] Mangeant, *loc. cit.*; cf. also Ceillier, *ibid.* 453.

[21] Mangeant, *loc. cit.*

[22] Cf. F. Cayré, *Précis de Patrologie* 2 (2nd ed., Paris 1933) 179; G. Fritz, " Pomère," *Dict. de théol. cath.* 12. 2 (1935) 2543.

[23] See below, n. 40. For further discussion of the elimination of Prosper as the author, cf. L. Valentin, S. *Prosper d'Aquitaine* (Toulouse 1900) 651-55.

[24] *Loc. cit.* The continuator of Gennadius says merely: Memini legisse me olim eius dictatum . . . et alium *de vitiis et virtutibus* praetitulatum.

[25] Cf. Ceillier, *op. cit.* 453; Mangeant, *loc. cit.*

[26] J. G. Pfister's German translation is the latest publication to attribute the treatise to St. Prosper: *Der hl. Prosper über das beschauliche Leben* (Würzburg 1826).

[27] Cf. J. Zellinger, " Pomerius," *Lex. f. Theol. u. Kirche* 8 (1936) 362. O. Bardenhewer, *op. cit.* 600, summarizes the contents of the treatise as follows: " Das Ganze ist . . . ein Vademecum, ein Lehr- und Erbauungsbuch für Kleriker, welches im ersten und zweiten Teile die Bahnen einer Pastoralanweisung einschlägt." Fritz, *loc. cit.*, approves of this summary, though he remarks by way of correction that the first two books, however applicable they may be to the clergy in general, are actually addressed to bishops only. See also the observations below, 179 n. 44.

[28] *Prosper de vita contemplativa atque actuali: sive de norma ecclesiasticorum* ([Speyer, Peter Drach] 1487). The translator examined a copy of this in the Union Theological Seminary Library, New York. The publisher and place of publication have been supplied: cf. M. B. Stillwell, *Incunabula in American Libraries* (New York 1940) P935.

[29] Arnold, *op. cit.* 83, counts as one factor contributing to the obscurity of the *De vita contemplativa* its " ill-suited and probably spurious title."

[30] M. Schanz—C. Hosius—G. Krüger, *Geschichte der römischen Literatur* 4. 2 (Munich 1920) 555; Cayré, *op. cit.* 2. 182.

[31] Cayré, *op. cit.* 2. 177, praises the firm moderation with which some delicate questions are handled in the treatise—a moderation that reveals the prudence and wisdom of the experienced writer.

[32] The continuator of Gennadius, who mentions only Book 3 of

the treatise, likewise places it at the end of his enumeration of Pomerius' works.

[33] Foreword to Book 2.

[34] Cf. Ceillier, *op. cit.* 453; Mangeant, *loc. cit.* For Julianus of Vienne, see Arnold, *op. cit.* 210.

[35] Cf. A. J. Festugière, *Contemplation et vie contemplative selon Platon* (Paris 1937).

[36] Cf. especially W. Völker, *Das Vollkommenheitsideal des Origenes* (Beitr. z. hist. Theol. 7, Tübingen 1931) 76 ff.; also A. Lieske, *Die Theologie der Logosmystik bei Origenes* (Münst. Beitr. z. Theol. 22, Münster i. W. 1938) 88, 134 f., *passim*.

[37] Hilary of Poitiers and Rufinus had done much to make Origen known in Gaul; cf. Arnold, *op. cit.* 50 f.

[38] Cf. *Conf.* 13. 18; *De civ. Dei* 19. 19; *De Trin.* 1. 17-21; etc. See below, 11; F. Cayré, *La contemplation augustinienne. Principes de la spiritualité de Saint Augustin* (Paris 1927).

[39] Cayré, *Précis de patrologie* 2. 178 n. 3.

[40] The style of the *De vita contemplativa* is treated by F. Dübner, *Nouvelle choix des PP. latins* 1 (Paris 1852) extract 22; F. Degenhart, *Studien zu Julianus Pomerius* (Progr. Eichstätt 1905); Sr. M. Agnes Cecile Prendergast, *The Latinity of the De Vita Contemplativa of Julianus Pomerius* (Cath. Univ. of Am. Patr. Stud. 55, Washington 1938). See also C. J. Armstrong's review of the last-named work in *Class. Weekly* 32 (1939) 211 f.

[41] For example, the descriptions of the proud and the vain in 3. 8 and 3. 10.

[42] Pomerius himself states that he dictated this work; cf. 2. 4. 1. Regarding the same method of composition as employed by St. Augustine with the same unfortunate results, cf. J. P. Christopher's note on *De catechizandis rudibus*, 15. 23: ACW 2 (1946) 119 n. 145.

[43] Forewords to Books 1 and 2; 1. 23; 3. 14; 3. 34.

[44] Pomerius is not a Ciceronian, but an exponent of the Second Sophistic. Cf. Armstrong, *loc. cit.*

[45] This is inferred from his treatment of certain Scripture passages: cf. Degenhart, *op. cit.* 3; Fritz, *loc. cit.* 2543. Arnold, *op. cit.* 83 n. 242, deduces the same from a statement of Ennodius, *Ep.* 2. 6.

[46] Cod. 18524b, 18565, 18609, and 18665 in the Königliche Hof- und Staatsbibliothek in Munich.

BOOK ONE

[1] Pomerius uses the word *rusticitas*, which is the opposite of *urbanitas*; in the words of Quintilian, *Inst. or.* 6. 3. 17: *Urbanitas dicitur, qua quidem significari video sermonem praeferentem in verbis et sono et usu proprium quendam gustum urbis et sumptam ex conversatione doctorum tacitam eruditionem, denique cui contraria sit* rusticitas. Regarding the author's confession, repeated at the end of the treatise (3. 34. 1), cf. the Introduction, 11.

[2] The expression is proverbial. Cf. Propertius, *Eleg.* 2. 10. 6: in magnis et voluisse sat est. See A. Otto, *Die Sprichwörter und sprichwörtlichen Redensarten der Römer* (Leipzig 1890) 362.

[3] Cf. 1 Cor. 8. 1.

[4] *Congregandis fratribus aut alendis. Congregari* could be thought of here as employed in the same sense as the earlier and more usual term *colligere* (*collectio, collecta*): to gather for divine services, especially the Eucharistic Sacrifice. However, from other passages in Pomerius it appears that the term should be interpreted otherwise. At the close of 2. 8 the question as formulated here is repeated verbatim: Utrum congregandis fratribus aut alendis expediat facultates Ecclesiae possideri an perfectionis amore contemni. The answer —*expedit facultates Ecclesiae possideri, et proprias contemni* (1. 9. 1)—is elaborated in the following chapters, 9-16. In this section the author asserts vigorously that the possessions of the Church should be used for the sustenance of the poor, *unde pauper victurus* (9. 1), whose patrimony they are, *patrimonia pauperum* (9. 2). But the poor spoken of principally by Pomerius are the clergy, those born poor or who laudably have made themselves poor by voluntarily giving up all their earthly goods: *clerici . . . quos pauperes aut voluntas aut nativitas fecit* (11). These are the *fratres* referred to as *congregandi* and *alendi*; and the problem for discussion is: whether it is good and desirable for a bishop to be actively engaged as a steward in administering the Church's possessions in order to provide for the common or community life (*congregandis*) and support (*alendis*) of his subordinates, the *clerici* who live *in fraternitate* with him under the same roof. This interpretation is given in greater detail in a study of *Pomeriana* prepared by one of the Editors, Dr. Plumpe, for *Vigiliae Christianae* (Oct. 1947).

[5] Cf. below, 192 n. 69.

⁶ Job 7. 1, quoted according to the Septuagint. The Vulgate reads: *The life of man upon earth is a warfare.*

⁷ For the history of the idea that Christ is the emperor and the Christians His soldiers, see A. Harnack, *Militia Christi* (Tübingen 1905); E. L. Hummel, *The Concept of Martyrdom according to St. Cyprian of Carthage* (Studies in Christ. Ant. 9, Washington 1946) 56-90. For the pre-Christian period, cf. H. Emonds, "Geistlicher Kriegdienst. Der Topos der *militia spiritualis* in der antiken Philosophie," *Heilige Überlieferung, Festgabe I. Herwegen* (Münster i. W. 1938) 21-50.

⁸ Cf. Job 37. 23.

⁹ Note the very effective wordplay: Ergo futura vita creditur *beate sempiterna* et *sempiterne beata*, ubi est *certa securitas, secura tranquillitas, tranquilla iucunditas, felix aeternitas, aeterna felicitas.*

¹⁰ *Alacer motus.* As St. Augustine states in the *Enchiridion* 91 (cf. L. Arand, ACW 3 [1947] 86), they will be without weight or encumbrance—*sine onere, difficultate*; they will have *tanta facilitas, quanta felicitas.* Cf. 1 Cor. 15. 43 ff.; and below, 1. 11.

¹¹ Even anterior to patristic usage the *civitas* concept is employed often in the Bible; for examples, cf. Ps. 45. 5; 47. 2, 3, 9; 86. 3; Heb. 11. 10, 16; 12. 2; 13. 14.

¹² Cf. 1 Cor. 15. 53.

¹³ Cf. Job 4. 18; Isa. 14. 12; Apoc. 12. 7-10.

¹⁴ Cf. J. P. Christopher's translation of Augustine's *De catechizandis rudibus*, ACW 2 (1946) 126 n. 191.

¹⁵ Cf. Mark 12. 25.

¹⁶ Cf. 1 Cor. 15. 53.

¹⁷ Cf. Tertullian, *Adv. Marc.* 3. 24; also below, 190 n. 50.

¹⁸ Cf. Heb. 13. 14.

¹⁹ Cf. Ps. 23. 4; 50. 12; Prov. 20. 9.

²⁰ Cf. Gen. 1. 27; 5. 1; Wisd. 2. 23; James, 3. 9.

²¹ Cf. Augustine, *Enchir.* 91; *De civ. Dei* 22. 20.

²² Etsi erit ibi distantia mansionum. Cf. John 14. 2: In domo Patris mei *mansiones* multae sunt. See Augustine's interpretation of these *mansiones*: *In Ioan. Ev. tract.* 67. 2.

²³ Cf. Matt. 22. 30; Mark 12. 25.

²⁴ Cf. 1 Cor. 13. 12.

²⁵ Cf. Rom. 8. 19.

²⁶ 1 Cor. 13. 9.

²⁷ *Ibid.* 13. 10.

²⁸ Wisd. 9. 15. Cf. Augustine, *De civ. Dei* 14. 3.

[29] 2 Cor. 5. 7.

[30] 1 John 4. 12.

[31] Matt. 5. 8.

[32] Cf. John 1. 45.

[33] Cf. Gal. 5. 24.

[34] Cf. Luke 9. 62.

[35] Cf. Phil. 3. 13 f.

[36] Cf. below, 3. 20. 2.

[37] Cf. Augustine, *De beata vita* 4. 32; *Retract.* 1. 2, 4.

[38] Cf. Augustine, *De civ. Dei* 14. 25.

[39] Cf. *ibid.* 19. 20.

[40] For examples in Holy Scripture, see Gen. 12. 7; 17. 1; 18. 1; 26. 2, 24; Exod. 3. 2; 3 Kings 9. 2; 2 Par. 7. 12. The problem is discussed by Augustine, *De civ. Dei* 10. 13. In *Enchir.* 59 he also speaks of angels appearing in human form, *ut non solum cernerentur, verum etiam tangerentur.* Regarding the Old-Testament appearances of God in human form—theophanies—the Fathers before St. Augustine almost universally believed that only God the Son thus manifested Himself. See J. Barbel, *Christos Angelos* (Theophaneia 3, Bonn 1941) 47-107. Augustine broke with this tradition. Cf. especially the second and third book of his *De Trinitate*, and M. Schmaus, *Die psychologische Trinitätslehre des hl. Augustinus* (Münst. Beitr. z. Theol. 11, Münster i. W. 1927) 20-22, 160-63. See also J. Lebreton, "Saint Augustin théologien de la Trinité. Son exégèse des théophanies," *Misc. Agostin.* 2 (Rome 1931) 821-36.

[41] Augustine, *De civ. Dei* 22. 17: Sed mihi melius sapere videntur, qui *utrumque sexum resurrecturum esse* non dubitant. *Non* enim *libido ibi erit,* quae confusionis est causa.

[42] Cf. Augustine, *De serm. Domini in monte* 1. 15. 41.

[43] The "garment of immortality," τὸ ἔνδυμα τῆς ἀφθαρσίας, is a favorite term of the early Christian writers. Cf. F. J. Dölger, *Sphragis* (Paderborn 1911) 193; the same, *Sol Salutis* (2nd. ed., Münster i. W. 1925) 370. The term goes back to Pythagorean circles of Egypt. See J. Quasten, "A Pythagorean Idea in Jerome," *Amer. Jour. of Philol.* 63 (1942) 207-15; W. J. Burghardt, "Cyril of Alexandria on 'Wool and Linen,'" *Traditio* 2 (1944) 484-86.

[44] Here the word *pontifices* is used. We have already met the term in the first sentence of the Foreword: mi domine studiosissime *pontificum.* It occurs again in the following passages: 1. 13. 2; 1. 15. 1; 1. 22. 1 (here also *pontificatus*); 1. 23 (twice); 2. 9. 1. The word is most important in determining the subjects of Pomerius' treatise,

the persons whose spiritual advancement and duties and failings are discussed in this unique work, particularly in the first two books. Pomerius speaks above all concerning the bishops of his time, not the clergy in general. Because the author frequently makes mention of *sacerdotes*, "priests," and because practically everything that he sets forth on the subject of pastoral responsibilities is eminently applicable to the parochial clergy of our own day, it is too readily asserted (e. g., by Bardenhewer: cf. above, 175 n. 27) that the *De vita contemplativa* was written as a pastoral instruction for the clergy; and because evidently the writer when speaking of *pontifices* and *sacerdotes* applies both terms to the same group of clerics, it is asserted (e. g., by Prendergast, *op. cit.* 101) that Pomerius calls a priest *pontifex* (in 2. 9. 1). But in all instances *pontifices* is a designation for bishops, as it always was among Christians before and after Pomerius. It is they who are referred to as *sacerdotes*, a usage that can be illustrated many times from Cyprian to Gregory of Tours— decades after the *De vita contemplativa* was written; for examples, cf. Du Cange, "Sacerdos," *Gloss. med. et inf. Lat.* 7 (ed. nova, Niort 1886) 254. The present observations are illustrated in detail from Pomerius' text and from historical considerations in a paper by Dr. Plumpe (cf. above, 177 n. 4).

[45] This recalls Horace's description of the greedy rich man, *Odes* 2. 18. 23 ff.: Quid quod usque proximos | *revellis agri terminos* et ultra | limites clientium | salis avarus?

[46] Cf. 2 Cor. 4. 4; 8. 23.

[47] Cf. Rom. 8. 17.

[48] Quasi *patres* meos audeam *docere*. The word *patres* is here used in the sense of a holy, spiritual fatherhood. Ecclesiastical superiors— bishops, abbots, etc.—were familiarly so termed because of their office of instructing, guiding, correcting, and consoling their subjects. Such a superior was a *father* to the Christian faithful, as can be seen from the very early testimony of the *Martyrium Polycarpi* (12. 2 Funk-Bihlmeyer). When Polycarp, aged bishop of Smyrna, had professed his faith in the stadium, the enraged people cried: "This is the teacher (διδάσκαλος) of Asia and the *father* of the Christians (πατὴρ τῶν χριστιανῶν)." The superior was also eminently the *father* of the ministers working under him. Already St. Paul calls Timothy his "beloved son in faith" (1 Tim. 1. 2) and St. Peter speaks of "my son Mark" (1 Peter 5. 13). Cf. Augustine, *De mor. Eccl. Cath.* 31. 67, regarding the *patres* among the cenobites; for further instances in later writers, including Caesarius of Arles, cf. Du Cange.

Gloss. med. et inf. Lat. 6 (1886) *s. v.* Read B. Steidle, "Heilige Vaterschaft," *Ben. Monatsschr.* 14 (1932) 215 ff.; the same, "Abba Vater," *ibid.* 16 (1934) 88 ff.

[49] St. Augustine (*Serm.* 138. 5) also calls Christ the Good Shepherd (cf. John 10. 11 ff.): *Pastor pastorum,* the Shepherd of shepherds.

[50] F. Degenhart, *op. cit.* 18, calls this Pomerius' finest figure. The metaphor *Ecclesia-navis* goes back to subapostolic times; cf. Ignatius of Antioch, *Pol.* 2. 3. It is known to Tertullian and Hippolytus of Rome and is used by Cyprian frequently. For Pomerius the bishop is a pilot of the ship of the Church: long before him Cyprian called Pope Lucius the *gubernator,* pilot or captain, of the *Navis Ecclesia* (cf. *Ep.* 61. 1). Among many other occurrences, note particularly the striking passages in the *Canones Ecclesiastici Apostolorum* 2. 7. 57. Note also Augustine, *In Ioan. Ev. tract.* 25. 5; *Enarr. in Ps.* 103, *serm.* 4. 5; *Serm.* 63. 1 ff.; 75. 3. 4. Cf. H. Rahner, *Griechische Mythen in christlicher Deutung* (Zurich 1945) 430-92. For the Church represented as a ship in ancient Christian art, see G. Stuhlfauth, "Das Schiff als Symbol der altchristlichen Kunst," *Riv. di archeol. crist.* 19 (1942) 111-41.

[51] Cf. Augustine, *De doctr. Christ.* 4. 27. 59 f.

[52] Cf. 2 Thess. 3. 9; 1 Peter 5. 3.

[53] Cf. 1 Cor. 6. 15; 12. 27; Eph. 5. 30.

[54] Cf. Mark 16. 16.

[55] Cf. Matt. 19. 28; Luke 22. 29 f.

[56] Isa. 7. 9, quoted according to the Septuagint. The Vulgate reads: *If you will not believe, you shall not continue.* Note the writer's lapse in attributing the passage to the Apostle (= St. Paul)! One manuscript seems to read *propheta* or *prophetia* for *Apostolo.*

[57] Ps. 35. 4.

[58] Rom. 10. 17. The Vulgate reads: *by the word of Christ.*

[59] *Ibid.* 10. 14; cf. Augustine, *Conf.* 1. 1.

[60] Cf. Mark 16. 16; James 2. 17.

[61] Rom. 10. 10.

[62] Cf. above, n. 51.

[63] That is, if he does not preach.

[64] 2 Cor. 12. 21.

[65] *Ibid.* 11. 29.

[66] Ezech. 33. 7. C. F. Arnold, *op. cit.* 122 and n. 364a, observes that the qualities of Caesarius' sermons—their outspokenness and stirring picturesqueness—remind us of the manner of the prophet Ezechiel; that it is not by mere chance that in discussions of the

duties of the clergy both he and his teacher, Pomerius, rèvert especially to Ezechiel; and that in the present section (20-22) Pomerius relies exclusively on that prophet for the Scriptural basis of his observations on pastoral obligations.

[67] Ezech. 33. 7.

[68] *Ibid.* 33. 8.

[69] Ezech. 3. 18.

[70] Quis . . . tam *saxei* pectoris, quis tam *ferreus.* This probably is a reminiscence of Pliny the Younger, who writes (*Ep.* 2. 3. 7) that one who has no desire to become acquainted with the rhetorician Isaeus is *saxeus ferreusque.*

[71] Ezech. 34. 2-5.

[72] *Ibid.* 34. 7-10.

[73] Ps. 54. 6 f.

[74] Cf. Prov. 20. 22; Lam. 3. 26; Mich. 7. 7.

[75] Cf. above, n. 44.

[76] Ezech. 33. 9.

[77] *Ibid.* 33. 3-5. The word *speculator,* " watchman," is introduced from v. 2.

[78] 2 Cor. 11. 6.

[79] Pomerius evidently is very familiar with St. Augustine's views on the matter of eloquence and style as set forth in his outline of homiletics in the last half of the third book and in the fourth book of the *De doctrina Christiana.*

[80] In Gaul the Christians were especially demonstrative during sermons. Sidonius relates (*Ep.* 9. 3. 5) that he shouted himself hoarse as he listened to the sermons of Faustus of Riez. Cf. Arnold, *op. cit.* 126; J. Zellinger, " Der Beifall in der altchristlichen Predigt," *Festgabe A. Knöpfler* (Freiburg i. Br. 1917) 403-15.—The injunction given here by Pomerius had been stated with equal vigor by St. Jerome, *Ep.* 52. 7 (*Ad Nepotianum*): Dicente te in ecclesia, non clamor populi, sed gemitus suscitetur. Lacrimae auditorum laudes tuae sint.

[81] See the last paragraph of this treatise.

[82] *Phalerati sermonis. Phalerati* suggests the metal disks worn on the breast as military decorations, as well as the trappings for the forehead and breast of horses. Cf. Malnory, *op. cit.* 21. Symmachus and Sidonius Appolinaris also use the word in reference to rhetorical ornamentation. In classical Latin we find Terence, *Phorm.* 3. 2. 16, employing the phrase *phalerata dicta*—" fine speeches."

[83] Cf. the passages quoted in the preceding discussion, Ezech. 33. 3-9; 34. 2-10.

[84] Cf. 1 Tim. 3. 2-4.

[85] Note the homoeoteleuta: si non *inflentur* . . . sed *graventur*; nec *honorari* se, sed *onerari*. . . . Observe also the play on words in the second pair.

[86] Cf. Rom. 8. 17. This sentence furnishes a companion picture to the description given above, 13. 2, of those priests who cannot share in the contemplative life. Note the similar grammatical construction employed in the two passages.

[87] Cf. Luke 1. 2.

BOOK TWO

[1] Cf. Eph. 6. 5 ff.; Titus 2. 9 f.; 1 Peter 2. 18; also 1 Cor. 1. 12 ff.; Eph. 5. 22-30.

[2] As John Chrysostom, *De sacerd.* 6. 4, puts it, the priest must show himself χρηστὸν καὶ αὐστηρόν (" both kind and severe "), according to the condition and disposition of those under his charge.

[3] Pomerius, like many early Christian writers, often speaks of man's sinfulness and his spiritual restoration in medical terms. For a very detailed comparison of the priest's care of souls with the physician's practice of medicine, read Gregory of Nazianzus, *Or.* 2. 16-34. Cf. also John Chrysostom, *loc. cit.*

[4] Cf. Exod. 30. 10; Lev. 6. 2-16; Num. 16. 46-48; 1. Par. 6. 49.

[4a] Cf. Ps. 50. 19.

[5] Cf. Gal. 2. 9; also Clement's *Epistle to the Corinthians* 5. 2, for which see J. A. Kleist's observation, ACW 1 (1946) 106 n. 26.

[6] Ezech. 3. 17.

[7] Acts 20. 25-28.

[8] It is curious to note that in the quotation Pomerius has just given from the Acts he inadvertently writes " the kingdom of Jesus Christ " for " the kingdom of God."

[9] Cf. Mark 12. 25.

[10] Acts 20. 27. Arnold, *op. cit.* 124, shows from the present paragraph, among others, to what extent Caesarius was indebted to Pomerius, his teacher, for the theory which he applied in his sermons.

[11] Compare with this St. Paul's words to the master of the converted fugitive slave Onesimus (Philem. 1. 15 ff.): Forsitan enim ideo discessit . . . ut aeternum illum reciperes: iam non ut servum,

sed pro servo *carissimum fratrem.* . . . The passage in Pomerius indicates that slavery still existed, although under the influence of Christianity the Roman emperors had passed a number of laws for the betterment of the slaves. As early as 316 Constantine gave Christian masters the power to liberate their slaves in church in the presence of the clergy and the people (*Codex Justin.* 1. 13. 1). Cf. P. Allard, *Les esclaves chrétiens* (6th ed. Paris 1914) 332 ff.; J. Manquoy, *Le christianisme et l'esclavage antique* (Liège-Paris 1927) 55 ff.; A. T. Geoghegan, *The Attitude towards Labor in Early Christianity and Ancient Culture* (Stud. in Christ. Ant. 6, Washington 1945) 103; 137; 145; 223 ff. We may note here, too, that Caesarius, Pomerius' pupil, showed a great interest in the lot of manumitted slaves, as is attested by the records of the Council of Agde (506) over which Caesarius presided: cf. cc. 7, 29 (Mansi 8. 325, 329 = Hefele-Leclercq 2. 2. 984, 991 f.).

[12] The Apostles and early Christians described themselves as "servants of Christ" and "servants in Christ." Cf. S. Weber, *Evangelium und Arbeit* (Freiburg i. Br. 1898) 97 f.; H. Rengstorf, "Die Christen als δοῦλοι Gottes und des Christus," in G. Kittel, *Theol. Wörterb. z. N. Test.* 2 (1935) 276-80.

[13] Cf. Eph. 6. 5-9; Titus 2. 9 f.; 1 Peter 2. 18.

[14] Acts 20. 28.

[15] Cf. Rom. 14. 1 and 15. 1.

[16] Heb. 13. 17. Note that Pomerius has *expedit*, "is expedient," for *non expedit*, "is not expedient," of the Vulgate.

[17] Cf. Clement's *Epistle to the Corinthians* 15. 1 (trans. by J. A. Kleist, ACW [1946] 1. 18): "Those whose peaceful intentions are but a mask."

[18] Cf. Isa. 10. 2; Matt. 23. 14; Luke 20. 47. Cf. St. Jerome's letter to Nepotian, *Ep.* 52. 6, 16. Pomerius seems to have been well acquainted (see also above, 182 n. 80; below, 187 n. 80) with this famous letter.

[19] 2 Tim. 4. 2.

[20] Rom. 15. 1. The Vulgate reads: *Now we that are stronger ought to bear the infirmities of the weak.*

[21] *Male dicaces in se.* Addressing Antony, Cicero says (*Phil.* 2. 78): populum etiam *dicacem in te* reddidisti.

[22] Cf. Gal. 6. 2.

[23] John 1. 29.

[24] Cf. Ezech. 18. 23; 33. 11; 1 Tim. 2. 4; 2 Peter 3. 9.

[25] Cf. Matt. 5. 29 f.; Mark 9. 42-46.

[26] Cf. Jer. 29. 23.

[27] Matt. 6. 12.

[28] Cf. Prov. 18. 17.

[29] It seems that Pomerius leaves it to the conscience of the cleric who committed mortal sins in secret to impose a penance upon himself without confessing his sins publicly. The reason is that public penance, which was demanded for such sins, created the canonical impediment of *irregularitas*. See Isidore of Seville's principle that penance should be performed in such a way, ut a sacerdotibus et levitis Deo tantum teste fiat, a ceteris vero adstante coram Deo solemniter sacerdote: *De eccl. off.* 2. 6 (PL 83. 802). Cf. B. Poschmann, *Die abendländische Kirchenbusse im frühen Mittelalter* (Breslau 1930) 158 ff.

[30] Eccli. 19. 28.

[31] Prov. 19. 5.

[32] *Congregandis fratribus aut alendis*: cf. above, 177 n. 4.

[33] Bishop of Nola (+ 431), to whom his revered teacher, the rhetorician and poet Ausonius, addressed three letters in an effort to win him from his resolve to receive baptism and to take leave of the world entirely. Paulinus' replies are preserved in his *Carmina* 10 and 11. Both St. Jerome and St. Augustine admired him greatly and both carried on correspondence with him.

[34] Archbishop of Arles (+ 499). He, too, exchanged letters with St. Augustine.

[35] *Vota*, that is, given to the Church by the vows or promises of the faithful.

[36] Osee 4. 8.

[37] Cf. Titus 2. 14.

[38] 1 Cor. 7. 32.

[39] 1 Tim. 6. 10.

[40] 1 Cor. 9. 13.

[41] *Ibid* 9. 14.

[42] *Ibid.* 9. 15.

[43] *Ibid.*

[44] I follow the reading of the manuscripts, *quos potest faciat suos*; Le Brun des Marettes-Mangeant wrote *quos potest vincere, victores faciat suos*. This would mean that covetousness conquers certain people and then makes them apostles, conquerors in its behalf. This seems a rather unusual thought, one which does not receive further development by Pomerius in what follows.

[45] That is, to joys that in the end bring only torturing grief.

⁴⁶ Cf. Deut. 10. 9; 32. 9; Jos. 13. 33; Ps. 72. 26; Eccli. 17. 15; 45. 27; Lam. 3. 24; Zach. 2. 12; and elsewhere.

⁴⁷ Ps. 118. 57.

⁴⁸ *Ibid.* 15. 5.

⁴⁹ Cf. Num. 18. 20, 23; Deut. 10. 9 and 18. 1.

⁵⁰ Cf. Deut. 12. 26; 1 Mac. 3. 49.

⁵¹ Cf. Exod. 22. 29; 25. 2; 35. 5; Lev. 2. 12; Deut., Kings, Esd. *passim.*

⁵² Cf. Num. 6. 14.

⁵³ Cf. Lev. 22. 2.

⁵⁴ Acts 4. 32.

⁵⁵ The Cynics, for example, and later the Stoics. Cf. the characterization of Diogenes of Synope in T. Gomperz, *Greek Thinkers* 2 (trans. by G. G. Berry, New York 1905) 155 ff. See M. Olphe-Gaillard, "Les philosophies de l'antiquité gréco-romaine," *s. v.* "Ascétisme," *Dict. de spir.* 1 (1937) 950-60.

⁵⁶ Pomerius is here thinking most probably of the Priscillianists, who had their stronghold in Gaul and were notorious for their rigorous asceticism and their condemnation of all worldly possessions.

⁵⁷ Cf. Gen. 1. 29 and 2. 9.

⁵⁸ The fruit of the tree of life is here regarded as a prefiguration of the Eucharist. For Methodius of Philippi, *Symp.* 9. 3, this fruit typified the fruit of faith.

⁵⁹ *Capax Dei.*

⁶⁰ Gen. 3. 10.

⁶¹ *Ibid.*

⁶² *Protectione divina nudati.* In the Latin the original meaning of *pro-tegere* is clearly felt: "to cover before or in front," "to cover over."

⁶³ Cf. Gen. 2. 25 and Augustine, *De civ. Dei* 14. 17; also *De pecc. mer. et remiss.* 32. 36.

⁶⁴ Cf. 2 Par. 24. 20, 24; Augustine, *De civ. Dei* 13. 15.

⁶⁵ Note the wordplay: ut qui *posse non mori* acceperant in natura, *non posse mori* consequerentur in gloria. This (observe also in the following: *non posse peccare*) is quite certainly a reminiscence of the same phrasings in Augustine, *Enchir.* 105: God wished to show: quam bonum sit animal rationale quod etiam *non peccare possit*; quamvis sit melius quod *peccare non possit*; to which there is the parallel of: minor fuit immortalitas . . . in qua *posset* etiam *non mori*, quamvis maiora futura sit in qua *non possit mori*. Cf. L. A. Arand, ACW 3 (1947) 100 and n. 344.

[66] *Propinaret ferale consilium*: the picture of the devil serving a poisoned cup.

[67] Gen. 3. 5. The Vulgate reads: *For God doth know that in what day soever you shall eat thereof, your eyes. . . .*

[68] 1 John 2. 15 f.

[69] Cf. 1 Peter 2. 21.

[70] 1 John 2. 6.

[71] Col. 3. 1.

[72] On the subject of abnegation see J. Guibert and R. Daeschler, " Abnégation," *Dict. de spir.* 1 (1937) 67-110.

[73] Gal. 5. 24.

[74] Col. 3. 5.

[75] Cf. 2 Kings 23. 16; 1 Par. 11. 16 ff.

[76] Cf. 3 Kings 17. 6.

[77] Eph. 5. 18.

[78] 1 Tim. 5. 23. Cf. Augustine, *De mor. Eccl. Cath.* 33. 72.

[79] Cf. E. Vacandard, " Carême," *Dict. de la théol. cath.* 2. 2 (1910) 1733. Socrates in his *Ecclesiastical History* (5. 22) says that many ate fish in Lent, some even ate birds, under the pretext that, according to Moses, birds took their origin from the sea. Malnory, *op. cit.* 208, remarks that *carnes* and *sanguis* were more heavily restricted than birds because, " as naturalists and mystics admit, fowl is less heavy to body and soul."

[80] Cf. Augustine's Lenten sermon, *Serm.* 207. 2: Videas enim quosdam pro usitato vino inusitatos liquores exquirere, et aliorum expressione pomorum, quod ex uva sibi denegant, multo suavius compensare; cf. also *Serm.* 210. 8. 10; *De mor. Eccl. Cath.* 31. 67; Jerome, *Ep.* 52. 12 (here *sorbitiunculae delicatae* = " exquisite drinks" are also mentioned).

[81] This is set forth in the anti-Manichaean writings of St. Augustine; e. g., *De mor. Manich.* 15. 36; *Contra Faust.* 6. 6-8.

[82] That is, through rigorous fasting and abstinence.

BOOK THREE

[1] Wisd. 1. 11. Cf. Augustine, *De civ. Dei* 19. 28; *Enchir.* 92 f.; *Serm.* 26. 1 *Guelferb.* (529 Morin).

[2] *Perpetue beata ac beate perpetua.*

[3] A negative turn is here given to the old proverb: *qui bene latet bene vivit*: cf. Ovid, *Trist.* 3. 4. 25; Horace, *Ep.* 1. 17. 10; also A. Otto, *op. cit.* 189.

[4] Rom. 14. 23. This passage also holds an important place in St. Augustine's discussions of whether the *infideles* are capable of practicing *virtutes*: *De nupt. et conc.* 1. 4; *Contra Iul. Pelag.* 4. 25 ff. If Pomerius denies any value to virtues practiced by pagans, he means supernatural value. St. Augustine holds the same opinion.

[5] 1 Cor. 3. 1 f. The Vulgate does not have " when I came to you."

[6] *Ibid.* 3. 3.

[7] For the contrast, *vivere secundum hominem—vivere secundum Deum*, see also Augustine, *De civ. Dei* 14.4; *Serm.* 97. 2. 2.

[8] I follow the reading of some manuscripts: *Qui si potuerit, est* (for *si potuerit esse*) *cum quibus vult.* . . .

[9] Matt. 10. 20.

[10] Ps. 80. 11.

[11] Eccli. 10. 15.

[12] Cf. Isa. 14. 12 ff.; Luke 10. 18; Apoc. 12. 8 f.

[13] That is—in the view of the ancients—the lower air. For the air considered as the medium in which the devil and evil spirits exist and ply their nefarious activities, cf. Eph. 2. 2: . . . *aliquando ambulastis . . . secundum principem potestatis aeris huius.* See *ibid.* 6. 12; Athanasius, *De Incarn.* 25; Augustine, *De Gen. ad litt.* 3. 15; 11. 33: . . . *peccatores angelos minime dubitemus detrusos tamquam in carcerem caliginis huius aeriae circa terras; De agone Christ.* 1; *Enchir.* 9. 28 (cf. L. A. Arand, ACW 3 [1947] 36 and n. 68).

[14] Ps. 24. 17.

[15] Rom. 5. 12.

[16] Cf. Augustine, *De civ. Dei* 14. 3: *corruptio corporis quae aggravat animam, non peccati primi est causa, sed poena; nec caro corruptibilis animam peccatricem, sed anima peccatrix fecit esse corruptibilem carnem.*

[17] Cf. 2 Cor. 12. 7.

[18] So Degenhart, *op. cit.* 33, conjecturing *severitas* on the basis of

the variant *securitas* in two MSS. not used by Le Brun des Marettes-Mangeant. Of course, in the contrast, the accepted reading, *maturitas*, yields practically the same meaning.

[19] Eccli. 10. 15.

[20] 1 Tim. 6. 10.

[21] Augustine, *op. cit.* 14. 3.

[22] Augustine, *De Gen. contra Manich.* 2. 8. 10: *Est mater omnium haereticorum superbia.*

[23] Cf. Acts 20. 24; 2 Tim. 4. 7.

[24] Pomerius continues to speak of pride as a disease (*morbus*). St. Augustine has the same conception of it: cf. *Serm.* 175. 1; *Enarr. in Ps.* 118, *serm.* 9. 2.

[25] Cf. James 3. 6.

[26] The Latin suggests Prudentius, *Hamart.* 302 f.

[27] *Professionis suae propositum*: with reference to the solemn baptismal confession or *profession* of faith. Cf. Augustine, *Conf.* 8. 2. 5.

[28] Cf. Prov. 29. 13.

[29] For the Canticle of Canticles, see Origen, *In Cant. Cant. prol.*, preserved in the translation by Rufinus: moneo et consilium do omni, qui nondum carnis et sanguinis molestiis caret neque ab affectu naturae materialis abscedit, ut a lectione libelli huius eorumque quae in eo dicuntur, penitus temperet. Aiunt enim observari etiam apud Hebraeos, quod nisi quis ad aetatem perfectam maturamque pervenerit, *libellum hunc ne quidem in manibus habere permittatur.* Continuing, Origen also mentions the other two Biblical books referred to by Pomerius and states (*ibid.*): that it has been handed down to him that among the Hebrews the youth was taught the entire Bible in one and the same course of instruction, but that four parts were reserved to be imparted later—*ad ultimum*: i. e. *principium Genesis*, in quo mundi creatura describitur, *et Ezechielis prophetae principia*, in quibus de Cherubim refertur, *et finem*, in quo templi aedificatio continetur, *et hunc Cantici Canticorum librum.* It is probable that Pomerius was acquainted with Origen's testimony through the translation by Rufinus of Aquileia. Note, however, that Origen does not say, as does Pomerius, that the entire Book of Genesis was prohibited reading. Gregory of Nazianzus, *Or.* 2. 48, also refers to the ancient Hebrew tradition reported by Origen. He states that certain parts of Scripture were withheld from readers who had not yet completed their twenty-fifth year, though he does not specify which parts were forbidden.

[30] for the phrasing, cf. Vergil, *Aen.* 7. 415; 10. 447; Lucan, *Phars.* 7. 291.

[31] Cf. Titus 1. 16.

[32] The language used here (et *in ipso totum genus humanum, velut in radice* fructum, naturae sponte *peccantis vitiatione corrupit*) recalls Augustine, who states concerning the first man (*Enchir.* 8. 26): *stirpem* quoque *suam, quam peccando in se tamquam in radice vitiaverat.* . . .

[33] Velut *amici in obsequio,* hostes in animo. This evidently harks back in part to the *vulgare proverbium* (Augustine in a letter to Jerome, *Ep.* 82. 31) as formulated by Terence, *Andr.* 68: *Obsequium amicos,* veritas odium parit. This was quoted by Cicero, Lactantius, Rufinus, and others. Cf. Otto, *op. cit.* 368.

[34] The idea of man turning evil to good—*malo bene uti*—is found often in the writings of St. Augustine. Thus, when a man gives up his life for another, he turns the evil of death to good (*De pecc. mer. et remiss.* 2. 28. 45). Cf. Mausbach, *op. cit.* 1. 10; 2. 180 f.; L. A. Arand's observations on Augustine, *Enchir.* 8. 27: ACW 3 (1947) 122 n. 66. See also the following note.

[35] Cf. especially Augustine, *De civ. Dei* 13. 5; 19. 10.

[36] Gen. 4. 13.

[37] Cf. Prov. 14. 30.

[38] Cf. Vergil, *Aen.* 3. 29 f.

[39] Cf. *ibid.,* 4. 499; also Ovid, *Trist.* 3. 9. 18.

[40] Cf. Ps. 68. 6; 89. 8.

[41] Cf. Deut. 10. 17; 2 Par. 19. 7.

[42] Cf. 1 Cor. 4. 5.

[43] Cf. Isa. 65. 1 and Rom. 10. 20.

[44] Matt. 22. 13.

[45] Isa. 66. 24; Mark 9. 44.

[46] The Latin has only *actione privari.* In the translation *actio* is taken in the pregnant sense of "doing good," "doing good works," as is also suggested by a variant in one of the manuscripts: *boni operis actione privari.*

[47] Cf. Ps. 26. 1; Mich. 7. 8; John 8. 12; 12. 35; 12. 46; 1 John 1. 5; etc.

[48] That is, beatific vision.

[49] Cf. Apoc. 2. 11; 20. 6, 14; 21. 8. See Augustine, *De civ. Dei* 19. 28; *Enchir.* 92 f.; *Serm.* 26. 1 *Guelferb.* (529 Morin).

[50] Cf. also 1. 1. 2; 1. 2; 1. 10. 1; 1. 12. 2; 3. 13; 3. 28. 2; 3. 31. 5. St. Augustine, too, is fond of calling heaven our homeland—*patria,*

patria caelestis: *De doctr. Christ.* 1. 9. 9; 1. 10. 10; *In Ioan. Ev. tract.* 30. 7; *Serm.* 91. 7. 9; 92. 3. 3; 103. 5. 6; 159. 1. 1. Note also the title of one of his sermons addressed to the catechumens: *De cantico novo et de reditu ad coelestem patriam ac viae periculis* (ML 40. 677 ff.). Earlier, St. Cyprian uses the same term for heaven: cf. the magnificent passage in *De mort.* 26. See Heb. 11. 16: Nunc autem meliorem (*patriam*) appetunt, id est, *caelestem*; above, 178 n. 17.

⁵¹ 1 Cor. 12. 31.

⁵² *Ibid.* 13. 1.

⁵³ *Ibid.* 13. 2.

⁵⁴ Cf. Augustine, *Cont. litt. Petil.* 2. 77. 172; *De unico bapt.* 7. 11; *In Ioan. Ev. tract.* 9. 8.

⁵⁵ The "living Sun" is God or Christ. For the history of this term, see F. J. Dölger, *Sol salutis* (2nd ed., Münster i. W. 1925).

⁵⁶ 1 Cor. 13. 3. The Vulgate has: *all my goods*.

⁵⁷ Gal. 5. 6.

⁵⁸ 1 Cor. 13. 4-7.

⁵⁹ Rom. 5. 5.

⁶⁰ 1 Tim. 1. 5.

⁶¹ Cf. Deut. 6. 5; Matt. 22. 37; Mark 12. 30; Luke 10. 27.

⁶² Cf. Matt. 5. 43.

⁶³ The exposition in this section quite certainly is modeled on St. Augustine's *De doctrina Christiana* (cf. 1. 27. 28).

⁶⁴ 1 John 2. 15.

⁶⁵ This recalls the conditions required by Cicero of true love in true friendship (*De amic.* 100): . . . nulla indigentia, nulla utilitate quaesita.

⁶⁶ Cf. Tob. 4. 16; Matt. 7. 12; Luke 6. 31.

⁶⁷ Cant. 2. 4.

⁶⁸ The moral allegory of the Two Ways or the crossroads was a favorite commonplace in Christian and pagan antiquity. See Lactantius, *Inst. div.* 6. 3, where he speaks of the ancient tradition according to which the pattern of human life resembles the letter "Y": during his youth, an individual's life runs an even course; but when he arrives at the threshold of manhood, the way he has been traveling divides and runs on in opposite directions; and he is faced with the quandary of which new way to follow—that of inactivity, ease, comfort, vice, or that of incessant effort, rugged action, virtue. Cf. also the same author, *Epit.* 59. The tradition referred to by Lactantius as having been propagated by ancient phi-

losophers and poets is best known from the celebrated fable of Hercules at the crossroads. In this narrative, as told by the sophist Prodicus of Ceos (cf. Xenophon, *Mem.* 2. 1. 21-34), the hero, confronted by a division of the road along which he has been going and by two women advancing towards him from the diverging paths, chooses to follow the one woman, modest and dignified and inviting him to a life of virtue, rather than to accept the solicitations of the other, enticing him to a life of pleasure and ease. Cf. also Cicero, *De off.* 1. 118.

In early patristic literature the theory of the Two Ways plays a very prominent role. It forms the first part (1-6) of the *Didache*: the way of life and the way of death. It constitutes the second part of the so-called *Letter of Barnabas* (18-21): the way of light and the way of darkness. The way of life and the way of death are further set forth in the paraphrase made of the *Didache* in the first part of the seventh book of the *Apostolic Constitutions*. These documents show to what great extent the teaching of morality in early Christianity followed the model of the Two Ways; and here Christ had of course gone before, Matt. 7. 13 f.: . . . *broad is the way that leadeth to destruction . . . and strait is the way that leadeth to life.*

⁶⁹ Regarding the four cardinal virtues—prudence, fortitude, temperance, justice—and their opposites: Aeschylus, *Septem* 610 (a verse expunged by Wilamowitz in his edition of Aeschylus), is perhaps the first who mentions these four virtues together. Plato saw in these virtues four kinds of virtues, whereas the Stoics regarded them as different manifestations of one and the same virtue. This fourfold division of the fundamental virtues is often found in Cicero: *De off.* 1. 15 ff.; *De fin.* 3. 25 ff.; *Parad. Stoic.* 3. 21 f.; *Part. orat.* 76 ff.; etc. Cf. J. Kunsemüller, *Die Herkunft der platonischen Kardinaltugenden* (diss. Munich 1935).

In Christian ethics and morality St. Augustine above all gave it a place. He had become acquainted with it as a young man through his reading of Cicero's *Hortensius*; cf. the fragment of this lost work preserved in the *De Trin.* 14. 12. It may be that in this matter Pomerius derived the *philosophorum sententia* directly from Cicero or from St. Augustine's writings. Regarding the latter, see also *De mor. Eccl. Cath.* 25; *De div. quaest.* 83. 31; *De lib. arb.* 1. 27; 2. 50, 52; *De civ. Dei* 19. 25; and for a proper appraisal of these passages, cf. J. Mausbach, *Die Ethik des hl. Augustinus* (2nd ed., Freiburg i. Br. 1929) 1. 207 ff. Concerning ancient " lists of virtues and vices," cf. A. Vögtle, *Die Tugend- und Lasterkataloge in Neuen Testament* (Neutest. Abh. 16, Münster i. W. 1936) 4 f.

[70] Antiquity made much of the mystical significance of certain numbers, especially in the interpretation of the Bible. The sacredness of the number 4 was seen in the following Scriptural passages: Gen. 2. 10 ff.; Dan. 7. 2 ff.; Apoc. 4. 6 ff. Passages in which the Fathers treated the same mystical number are: Victorinus, *De fabr. mundi* (3. 456 Routh); Ambrose, *Hexaem.* 4. 9. 34; *De Abrah.* 2. 9. 65; Jerome, *In Ev. Matt.* 2. 15. 33; Augustine, *Enarr. in Ps.* 6. 2; *Serm.* 252. 10. 10; etc. Cf. J. Sauer, "Zahlensymbolik," *Lex. f. Theol. u. Kirche* 10 (1938) 1025-30; H. Lesêtre, "Nombre," *Dict. de la Bible* 4 (1908) 1677-97; for Pomerius, O. Zöckler, *Die Tugendlehre des Christentums . . . , mit besonderer Rücksicht auf deren zahlen-symbolische Einkleidung* (Gütersloh 1904) 93-95.

[71] These four emotions or "affections" (*affectiones*) are: desire (*cupiditas*), joy (*laetitia*), fear (*metus*), and sadness (*tristitia*). Cf. Augustine, *De civ. Dei* 14. 6 ff.; *In Ioan. Ev. tract.* 46. 8.

[72] Cf. Gen. 2. 10.

[73] Cf. Ezech. 1. 7-23.

[74] Cf. Augustine, *Enarr. in Ps.* 103, *serm.* 4. 14: Nolite vobis tribuere fortitudinem. *Si vestra est*, inquit, et mea non est: *duritia est*, non fortitudo; also *De mor. Eccl. Cath.* 22. 41.

[75] Matt. 5. 10.

[76] Exod. 15. 2; Ps. 117. 14; Isa. 12. 2.

[77] Cf. Phil. 3. 9; Augustine, *Op. imperf. cont. Iul.* 2. 158; *In Ioan. Ev. tract.* 50. 6; also Cicero, *De off.* 1. 7. 23: *Fundamentum autem est iustitiae fides.*

[78] Cf. Terence, *Heaut.* 77: Homo sum: humani nil a me alienum puto. This sententious verse was often quoted or alluded to: cf. Cicero, *De off.* 1. 9. 30; *De leg.* 1. 12. 33; Seneca, *Ep.* 95. 53; Ambrose, *De off.* 3. 7. 45; etc. See Otto, *op. cit.* 165 f.

[79] In the passage cited in the previous note, St. Ambrose, discussing the unfair treatment of strangers, argues the opposite: namely, that beasts do have consideration for their kind and give mutual assistance among themselves.

[80] Chapters 1 and 2.

[81] 1 Cor. 15. 28; cf. Augustine, *De civ. Dei* 19. 20; 22. 30.

[82] *Tamquam verus agricola in agro suo.* St. Augustine likewise calls God the *agricola*, the farmer who tills and waters the soil of our soul and receives our good works as His harvest: cf. *Enarr. in Ps.* 66. 1; 102. 4; *Conf.* 2. 3. 5. The inspiration for this beautiful

metaphor comes from St. Paul, 1 Cor. 3. 7-9: . . . *Dei agricultura estis*, Dei aedificatio estis.

83 *Qui sit habitator noster.*

84 Pomerius refers to the Peripatetics and Stoics. Cf. Augustine, *De civ. Dei* 9. 4; 14. 8.

85 Cf. Augustine, *ibid.* 19. 4.

86 Augustine, *ibid.* 9. 4: Duae sunt sententiae philosophorum de his animi motibus, quos Graeci πάθη, nostri autem quidam, sicut Cicero (*De fin.* 3. 10. 35; *Tusc. disp.* 3. 4. 7) *perturbationes*, quidam affectiones vel affectus, quidam vero, sicut iste de Graeco expressius, *passiones* vocant.

87 Cf. Augustine, *ibid.* 19. 19, where he also quotes St. Paul: 1 Tim. 3. 1: Qui episcopatum desiderat, bonum opus desiderat.

88 Cf. Matt. 2. 2; 27. 11; Mark 15. 2; John 18. 37; 1 Tim. 6. 15; etc. For the New Testament concept of Christ as King, cf. K. L. Schmidt, "βασιλεύς," "βασιλεία," in G. Kittel's *Theol. Wörterb. z. Neuen Test.* 1 (1933) 577-79, 581 f. The Fathers, particularly St. Augustine, have developed fully the idea of Christ's kingship.

89 This is the original, etymological meaning of the old Roman word *prudentia < pro-videntia*, from *pro* (= *prae*)-*videre*: a "foreseeing" and "providing against." It is this eminently practical and useful prudence and wisdom, as contrasted with Greek book wisdom and scientific knowledge, which Cicero throughout his writings claims for the *Romani antiqui*, the ancestors who had made Rome mistress of the world. Cf. J. C. Plumpe, *Wesen und Wirkung der auctoritas maiorum bei Cicero* (diss. Münster: Bochum-Langendreer 1935) esp. 32-48 (*prudentia, sapientia*).

90 Cf. James 1. 12; Augustine, *De civ. Dei* 9. 5.

91 Matt. 10. 16.

92 Ps. 18. 13 f.

93 Cf. Augustine, *Enchir.* 22. 81: Duabus ex causis peccamus, aut nondum videndo quid facere debeamus; aut non faciendo, quod debere fieri iam videmus. Quorum duorum illud *ignorantiae* malum est, hoc *infirmitatis*. See L. A. Arand, ACW 3 (1947) 136 n. 278.

94 Ps. 26. 1.

95 Cor. 13. 9 f.

96 This reference is to the Stoics and their doctrine of apathy.

97 2 Cor. 11. 3. The Vulgate reads *a simplicitate* for *a castitate*. The best manuscripts of the original Greek have both: ἀπὸ τῆς ἁπλότητος καὶ τῆς ἁγνότητος. We make the curious observation that in St. Augustine, who usually reads *a castitate*, we find both versions

within the same treatise: *In Ioan. Ev. tract.* 8. 4, *a simplicitate et castitate; ibid.* 13. 12, *a castitate.*

[98] Phil. 1.23. The Vulgate has *desiderium habens* for *cupio.*

[99] This title St. Paul uses himself, 1 Tim. 2. 7: in quo positus sum ego praedicator et apostolus (veritatem dico, non mentior) *doctor gentium* in fide et veritate.

[100] Rom. 9. 2 f.

[101] *Ibid.* 16. 19.

[102] 2 Tim. 3. 3.

[103] Ps. 121. 1.

[104] *Ibid.* 68. 21.

[105] Eccli. 1. 27.

[106] Wisd. 6. 21.

[107] Cf. Augustine, *De civ. Dei* 14. 6.

[108] Cf. above, 194 n. 84.

[109] See M. Olphe-Gaillard, " Stoicisme," *s. v.* " Ascétisme," *Dict. de spir.* 1 (1937) 953-7; J. Stelzenberger, *Die Beziehung der früh-christlichen Sittenlehre zur Ethik der Stoa* (Munich 1933).

[110] Cf. Matt. 26. 37; Luke 19. 41; John 11. 35.

[111] Cf. Heb. 4. 15; 2 Cor. 5. 21; John 8. 29, 46; 14. 30; 1 John 3. 5; Tertullian, *De an.* 41: Solus Deus sine peccato, et solus homo sine peccato Christus, quia et Deus Christus; *De carne Christi* 16; Hippolytus, *Cont. Noet.* 17; Gregory of Nazianzus, *Or.* 30. 21; 38. 13; John Chrysostom, *In 1 Cor. hom.* 38. 2. Cf. L. Atzberger, *Die Unsündlichkeit Christi* (Munich 1883).

[112] The Academic Crantor of Soli, quoted by Cicero, *Tusc. disp.* 3. 6. 12. Crantor wrote a treatise *On Sorrow,* on which Cicero drew extensively in the third book of the *Tusculan Disputations* and on which he modelled his own *De consolatione,* written soon after his daughter's death in 45 B. C.

[113] Ps. 18. 10.

[114] 1 John 4. 18.

[115] Eccli. 1. 28.

[116] 1 John 4. 18.

[117] Eccli. 7. 14.

[118] Cicero, *In Cat.* 1. 2. 4.

[119] Vergil, *Aen.* 6. 733, also quoted by St. Augustine in a similar discussion: *De civ. Dei* 14. 3.

[120] Ps. 31. 11.

[121] Cf. Augustine, *De civ. Dei* 14. 6.

[122] This tribute to St. Augustine and his teaching is particularly

noteworthy: though coming from a fellow African, it was written in territory that still heard Augustine accused of heresy. It was here that John Cassian became the father of semi-Pelagianism, which in Pomerius' day was still strong in the Rhone country. Pomerius' estimate of St. Augustine also contradicted the opinion of other eminent opponents of Augustinism, such as Vincent of Lerins and Faustus of Riez.

[123] *De civ. Dei* 14. 9.

[124] *Ibid.*

[125] 1 John 4. 18; cf. above, 3. 31. 3.

[126] Cf. Ps. 18. 10 and above, 3. 31. 3.

[127] Cf. Augustine, *De mus.* 6. 16. 51, 55. In *Ep.* 155. 3. 12 he states that in the blessed afterlife these virtues will no longer be needed, that they unite into one virtue; cf. *ibid.* 16.

[128] Cf. Gal. 5. 17.

[129] Ubi *in aenigmate* quodam prudentes *illuminat*—probably with reference to 1 Cor. 13. 12, in which St. Paul contrasts our present seeing with the beatific vision: Videmus nunc per speculum *in aenigmate*; tunc autem facie ad faciem.

[130] James 1. 5.

[131] Degenhart, *op. cit.* 2, deduces from this that Pomerius was self-taught. See the Introduction 11 f.

[132] This recalls a well-known chapter in St. Augustine: *De doctr. Christ.* 4. 28.

[133] St. Augustine, *ibid.*, has a similar sententious statement regarding the teacher and the words he uses in teaching: Nec doctor verbis serviat, sed verba doctori.

INDEX

INDEX

Aaron, 59
abnegation, 187
abstemiousness, 96
abstinence, nature of, 6, 9; perfection in, 16, 85-87, 114; spiritual, 100; 106, 109, 126 f., 140, 145
actio, 190
action, 122, 134, 154, 157, 165, 191
actione privari, 190
active life, 6-9, 11, 15, 31-33, 52-54, 100, 154
activity, and contemplation, 9; spiritual, a burden to the carnal-minded, 114; 188
Acts of the Apostles, 60, 86
Adam, saw God as Patriarchs did, 88; man born carnally of, 91; not to be imitated, 91; 143
administrators, ecclesiastical, 156
admonitions, of priests, 47. See correction
adulterer, adultery, 77, 111, 117
adversity, borne by Christ, 28, 92; 28, 125, 147, 158
advice, spiritual, 46
Aeonius, bishop of Arles, 4
Aeschylus, *Septem* 610: 192
affectation, of style to be avoided by teachers, 50
affection(s), of the flesh, 23; of religious pretenders, 64; of Christ for sinners, 68; 144, 193
affliction, 140
Africa, 3, 4, 173

afterlife, 36, 196. See heaven, homeland
Agde, council of, 184
age, old, 22; unknown in paradise, 88; Christian, 84
agitations, 162. See disorders, passions
agreement, faith in a mutual, 62
agricola, God as, 193
air, gloomy, 107; lower, 188
Aix-la-Chapelle, synod of, 174
alacer motus, 178
Allard, P., 184
allurements, 136, 140
alms, of the poor, 77
almsgiving, 105, 126, 134
altar, 70 f., 79
ambition, to be avoided, 37; 93, 111, 125, 142, 147
Ambrose, St., and pastoral instruction, 173
    De Abrah. 2. 9. 65: 193; *De off.*, 173; 3. 7. 45: 193; *Hexaem.* 4. 9. 34: 193
ancients, the, 116, 143, 154
angels, assembly of, 19; dignity of, 24; happiness of, 31; man will gain likeness to 33, 61; judgment of holy and wicked, 20 f.; became devils through pride, 107, 109; the devil and his, 130; 132
anger, of God, 72; of the insolent, 71; 32, 93, 109, 135
Angers, 7
animosity, 93

76, 82, 123, 126-29, 132, 134, 136-38, 148 f., 159 f., 162-64, 166. See evil, vices

sin offerings, 84

sincerity, 135

sinfulness, man's, 183; in others overlooked by carnal priests, 44

sinlessness, in heaven, 22

sinners, differ in kind, 57; honored by carnal priests, 44; 22, 67 f., 73, 123, 127, 129, 150, 161

Sirmond, J., 5, 7

slavery, slaves, 61, 85, 124, 183 f.

sleep, 88, 115

sloth, 109

sobriety, 109

socialis virtus, 11

society, of the saints, 130; human, 122, 149, 155 f.

Socrates, *Ecclesiastical History* 5. 22: 187

soldiers, of Christ, 18, 79, 178

solicitude, 79 f., 84

Son, the, generated by the Father, 39; 179

son(s), beloved in faith, 180; of Levi, 83; 137

song, 115

sorrow, unknown in heaven, 22; 28, 79, 122, 140, 142, 147, 158, 162, 165

soul, cast to earth by love of things below, 24; oppressed by body, 25; the four emotions of, 143, 161-65; corporeality of, argued in Pomerius' *De anima*, 174; 47, 59, 62 f., 65, 69, 74, 76, 78, 85 f., 103, 109, 112 f., 114 f., 121, 123-25, 127, 135-37,

139 f., 148, 150, 153 f., 167, 187

soundness, perfect, in heaven, 22 f.

speculator, 182

speech, 49, 58, 114, 118 f., 122, 125

Spirit, of the Father, 106; 160. See Holy Spirit

spirit, the, to be obeyed by the body, 31, 96, 137; in heaven its struggle with the flesh will cease, 167; 19, 59, 81, 107, 112, 142, 153, 167

spirit(s), evil, 20, 33, 38, 44, 82, 188

Steidle, B., 181

Stelzenberger, J., 195

stewards, of heaven, 59; of a church's possessions, 72 f., 77; bishops as, 177

stewardship, of priests, 85

Stillwell, M. B., 175

Stoics, 162, 164, 186, 192, 194

stomach, restored by food, 95; helped by wine, 95; fastidious, 96

strangers, treatment of, 32, 51, 193; to heaven, 33; and kinsfolk, 137

strength, 86, 125, 131, 136, 141, 147, 168

struggle, 111, 166

studies, 28, 34, 73

Stuhlfauth, G., 181

stupidity, of the worldly wise, 161

style, of the *De vita contemplativa*, 11; ornate, to be avoided by teachers, 50; Augustine's